UFFCULME
A Culm Valley Parish

Published by the
Uffculme Local History Group

1988

First published in 1988
by
THE UFFCULME LOCAL HISTORY GROUP
18 The Square, Uffculme, Devon EX15 3AA

Designed, typeset and printed in Great Britain
by
MASLANDS LTD.
16a Fore Street, Tiverton, Devon. (0884) 252613

All rights reserved. No part of this publication may be reproduced, stored in a retrieval system or transmitted in any form or by any means without prior permission of the copyright holder.

©1988. The Uffculme Local History Group

British Library Cataloguing in Publication Data

Uffculme: a Culm valley parish.
  1. Devon. Uffculme
  I. Uffculme Local History Group
  942.3'54

ISBN 0-9513111-0-7

ACKNOWLEDGEMENTS

THIS publication consists of contributions by members of the Group and by distinguished authorities, Dr C A Ralegh Radford, its President, and Dr Chris Brooks of the University of Exeter. Their support is greatly valued.

The Group acknowledges the generous help given by many people who have lent documents and photographs. Particular thanks are due to the staff of the Devon County Record Office for their expert guidance and for permission to reproduce some of the sketches by Peter Orlando Hutchinson. The reproduction of a number of old and faded photographs has been possible through the skill of Charles Stokes who gave freely of his time for several photographic assignments. George H Hall kindly gave permission for use of some of his photographs of St Mary's Church. The plan of Bradfield House is reproduced by kind permission of the Royal Archaeological Institute.

The book is not intended to be a complete history of the parish but rather a selection of accounts of its past. The views expressed are those of the individual contributors to whom queries should be addressed direct. No responsibility is accepted for omissions or errors.

Gordon A Payne, Editor.

SPONSORS

THE following organisations sponsored the project with generous donations that enabled the Group to proceed to publication with confidence. The timely help is acknowledged with thanks.

Clark's Motors (Cullompton) Ltd
Lloyd Maunder Ltd
The Uffculme Trust

SUBSCRIBERS

The following individual subscribers helpfully supported the project with their contributions in advance of publication:

Sheila Abraham
Mr & Mrs C R Amor
Phyllis C Andrews
Mr R F Andrews
A W Ashworth
Mrs J B Austin
W J C Baigent
Mr A F Baker
H & F E Baker
Dr & Mrs Peter Baker
Richard & Louise Bancroft
M Bardsley
Arthur & Madge Bates
Mr Ian Anthony Bath
Mrs Patricia Batson
Mrs W E Battersby
Janet Baty (Dargaville, NZ)
John Baysham
L A Becker
Bill Berry
Leslie Billett
G Bisiker
M V & G Boizot
Mrs Jessie May Bradon
John Brayne-Baker
Roy & Gwen Britton
Mr & Mrs R J Brooks
D A Brown
Mrs S L Brown
K J Burrow
Betty Bussell
Hester Butler
Michael I R Bull
Adrian Cadbury
Mrs S M Callaghan
Mrs E Carr
Freda E Carter
John Caudle
R W & M C Chambers
Tony J Charlton
Miss K E Clarke
E W Clitsome
Phil & Hilary Cole
J F Collins

Mr & Mrs S Collins
Philip & Linda Cornish
Mrs M Cousin
Felicity Cowley
Mr & Mrs Brian A Creed
Culm Valley Activities Centre
C Q W Cumbes
P M Cumbes
Q J Cumbes
Kate Delamain
Mrs Bessie Denner
Reg Denner
Marc Deville (St Quentin, France)
Devon & Exeter Institution Library
Clare Dorrington
Mr & Mrs W Drayner
W Driver
David Edmund
Mrs Ron Edwards
Exeter Rare Books
The Fisher Family
B Fitzpatrick
Mrs Joy Foot
Peter Fowler
Rev'd & Mrs Geoffrey Fraser
Ray Gale
Jill Gardener
Iris H M Gearing
Pamela Gibbs
Mrs J Gidney
Michael C Gilgrist
Mrs Molly Goodhart
B Gordon
Bernard Gough (Dargaville, NZ)
Mr J Green
Mr T R Green
Mrs J Greet
Mrs J Grierson
D H Haddock
D E Hagley
H W D Hagley
Clifford Harding
E Hare
Mr R Harvey

Mr J F Heath
Alan & Cathy Hempstead
Joan Hepworth
Pam & Chris Hicks
Mrs Dorothy Alma Hine
Rachel Hitchcock
Dr J Hofmann
Neil David Holmes
Trevor William Holmes
Tom Holway
Mr Alan T Hooker
Mr W J Hookway
Terry Horn
E Howard-Williams
Mr R E Hunt
J M Huntley-Jones
Michael Hutchings
Mr C Hutchison
Margaret James
Sarah Jarman
Mr & Mrs W T Jones
Mrs C M Jenkyns
Spencer & Pam Kingdon
Joy Knight
Dr P Knight
Peggy M Knowlman
Mr A Lawson
Rosemary Lamyman
Miss R L Lee
Jocelyn LeRoux
Mrs C Lewis
Clive Loader
Keri G Long
Stephen Luxton
Mary Mackenzie
Alison Manuel
Mrs Christine Marsh
Joanna Mattingly
Mrs Margaret Maunder
Robin Maxwell-Hyslop MP
Roy & Denise Middleton
Mrs G E Mitchell
Chris Mumford
Kathleen Mundy
Peter H Newton
Mrs Ida M Norton
Barbara Oates
Frank Oates
The Old Well

Charles Iain Oliver
Frances Ridley Oliver
Lindsey Frances Oliver
Dorothy Ellen Palfrey
Andrew Pardoe
Julie Pardoe
Mrs Jenny Parsons
Gordon Payne
Jean Payne
Kim Pearce
Mark Pearce
C Pengilley
L Pengilley
Mr & Mrs R Pettifer
Stuart W Phillips
Mike & Valerie Pollard
Mrs B R Potts
Mrs P Power
Mr D L Pugh
David Pugsley
Philip R Pullman
Mr Phil Pyne
T & H Radmore
Paul & Ann Read
Mrs A H Reed
A J H Reed
Mr D G Regardsoe
James H Reid
Miss M J Retter
Mrs S J Retter
Mrs F Rew
Mr W S Robertson
Edna K Robinson
G W Ross
Peter Sainsbury
Pat & Anne Salter
Miss A Sampson
Miss C Sampson
Col C W Saunders ret'd
Mrs E M Saunders
Rev'd Elaine Seale
Rupert W K Sheddick
J & T M Shere
Dorothy & Michael Shewell
Mrs Jeanette Simmons
P Silk
Doreen Snipes
Bertie Sömme
Nick & Nancy Soultanian

(continued)

Mrs F Stamp
Rev'd Leo Stephens-Hodge
Mrs D Struck
G R Swales
George Tatham
Avril G Taylor
Rita & Tony Taylor
Wm J Thomas
Valerie & Arthur Thorning
David Trist
Miss M Tucker
Mrs M L Turpin (née Norton)
Mrs Mary Twiddy
1st Uffculme Guides
Uffculme School
Alan P Voce

Isabel Weeks
Jillian Weldon
Francis & Sue Welland
David & Sarah Wells
Mr & Mrs D V Whitby
Edward White
Thomas Edward White
Gladys Ellen Williams
V Williams
S A Wint
Graham Winterbourne
Mrs Ivy V Wood
Miss Christine E Wright
Sylvia Wroath
P Yeo
Mr & Mrs L C Young

Contributions were also received in memory of:

Honorary Alderman William John Denner
Samuel Denner

CONTENTS

MEDIEVAL UFFCULME by Dr C A Ralegh Radford	9
A VICAR REFLECTS: THE REV'D JAMES WINDSOR by Adrian Reed	15
NICHOLAS AYSHFORD'S GIFT TO UFFCULME by Elaine Seale	21
UFFCULME DURING THE EARLY VICTORIAN YEARS by Pat Regardsoe	24
BRADFIELD by Dr C A Ralegh Radford	42
THE VICTORIAN RESTORATIONS OF UFFCULME CHURCH by Dr Chris Brooks	48
THE BAPTIST CHURCH by Christine Snell	58
UFFCULME UNITED REFORMED CHURCH by Margaret Batting	59
TRADE AND INDUSTRY IN UFFCULME, 1850-1939 by Adrian Reed	61
COLDHARBOUR MILL by Linda Cracknell	66
UFFCULME WORDS AND DIALECT by Jack Gollop	71
INNS, TAVERNS AND BREWING IN THE PARISH OF UFFCULME by Jack Gollop	76
GRANTLANDS by Pamela Gibbs	79
THE US 17th FIELD ARTILLERY AT GRANTLANDS by Gordon Payne	83
THE CULM VALLEY LIGHT RAILWAY by Jack Gollop	84
CRICKET IN UFFCULME by Jack Gollop	89
UFFCULME UNITED CHARITIES TRUST by Col C W Saunders	94
GREGORY CREASE, PHOTOGRAPHER by Gordon Payne	97
AN ENERGETIC PARSON: THE REV'D HENRY BRAMLEY by Adrian Reed	100
UFFCULME IN 1905 by C N (Charlie) Levett	102
A VISITOR'S VIEW OF UFFCULME IN 1849 by Adrian Reed	109
MAP OF THE PARISH	114

Part of the Map of the County of Devon by Benjamin Donn, published 1765.
The complete map was reprinted in facsimile by the Devon and Cornwall Record and the University of Exeter in 1965 to mark the bicentenary.

MEDIEVAL UFFCULME
by Dr C A Ralegh Radford

UFFCULME means Uffa's farm (or Uffa's settlement) on the Culm. The name is the same as Offa and older forms of the name (eg in the Domesday Book) are spelt with an initial 'O'. Offa was the greatest of the Mercian kings (ie of the Midlands). He reigned from 757 to 796. He claimed descent from Offa, a king in Angeln (modern Schleswig), a folk hero who figures in the earliest Anglo-Saxon poetry. The name of the river, 'Culm', is derived from a British word meaning knot or loop; hence, the winding river.

The Village

Uffculme is one of a number of compact or nucleated villages found all over Devon, but more frequently east of the river Exe. They represent the earliest Saxon settlements of the late seventh or eighth centuries, when the rising power of Wessex conquered the land from the British. The characteristic plan is of a large square or rectangle, left open for meetings and markets, with houses set along each side in front of yards or gardens. The parish church usually stands at one side or at the end, a little retired. Such nucleated settlements were usually surrounded by open fields laid out in strips and traces of this arrangement may be seen in the park at Bridwell and also within the parish. The overall pattern has been obliterated by early enclosure.

These settlements were important centres of population usually held directly by the king and they often became the centres of 'hundreds' when these were organized in the tenth century. Uffculme was given by Athelwulf, King of Wessex (839-855), to Glastonbury Abbey. It was then an estate of twenty four hides.

In a later document the gift is described as the manor with the churches and chapels. The estate was probably larger than the present parish, perhaps extending as far west as the Spratford stream, just west of the former Tiverton Junction station. The earliest description of the estate is in the Domesday Book (1086), as follows

'Walscin (Walter of Douai) has a manor called Offecoma (Uffculme) which Edith held in 1066 and it paid geld for fourteen hides. There is land for thirty ploughs. Walscin has in hand five hides and two ploughs; the villeins have nine hides and fifteen ploughs. There are forty five villeins and six bordars and six serfs and one pack-horse and fourteen head of cattle and two swineherds, who render fifteen swine, and two hundred sheep and ten goats and two mills which pay ten shillings rent and twenty five acres of coppice and twenty five acres of meadow and sixty acres of pasture. It is worth annually twelve pounds and it was worth ten pounds when Walscin received it.'

A 'hide' was roughly 120 acres of ploughland. There was also much waste affording rough pasture, and woodland providing fuel and grazing for the swine. The ordinary small village was rated at five hides and had about one quarter of the number of inhabitants that Uffculme had. The villeins were ordinary farming tenants, the bordars were small holders and the serfs were landless labourers.

Domesday Book records that Uffculme belonged to Walter of Douai who was a Flemish follower of William the Conqueror. In 1066 he had married Edith, the holder, who was a widow. In law, she was only a life-tenant. In or about 1050 the Abbey of Glastonbury, which needed ready money to meet taxes and other out-goings, had granted a lease for life to Edith. She paid seven marks of gold down and when she died the manor would have reverted to the Abbey, to which she also promised to bequeath two precious reliquaries of relics. It was a normal though dangerous practice and the Abbey took special precautions. The arrangement was guaranteed by the King and there were sixteen sureties for performance, including Edith's son by her first marriage, who was probably a minor. But Walter got a grant from King William and kept the property when Edith died. This was of doubtful legality. He passed it on to his son, which was illegal.

In 1136, the Abbot of Glastonbury was Henry of Blois, a brother of King Steven. He drove a hard bargain with Stephen in return for his support and Uffculme was returned to Glastonbury. They did not hold it for many years. Robert, the heir of Walter of Douai and then holder, led a revolt against Stephen but was forced to surrender after Uffculme had been ravaged and the manor house burnt in the course of the fighting. Eventually, however, the property returned to the lay owner and was no more connected with Glastonbury. Robert of Bampton, the descendant of Walter of Douai, who held the property in the time of Stephen, left a daughter Juliana, who married William Paynel. Their son was Fulk Paynel. From the Paynels the property descended to the Cogans and then to Sir Hugh Courtenay and so to the Earls of Bath. The Lords of the Manor were not resident, so the manor house would have been a simple building, acting as an estate office and for the holding of the manor court. Its site is not known.

Medieval Farms

Smithencott, the Smith's small holding or cottage, is mentioned in 1223. Skinner's Farm is named from William Skinner (1333).

Gaddon House, a goat farm or goat hill, is mentioned in 1249. Goodleigh, Hayne, Northcott and Rull are all named in 1249. Woodrow was the home of John atte Wood in 1330.

The Church

The first mention of the church is in the charter of 1136, returning the property to Glastonbury. The plural reference to church*es* may be a mistake, but possibly Burlescombe was once a part of Uffculme. One of the chapels referred to was probably that at Bodmiscombe, later the centre of a small estate held by the Hospitallers, though they did not acquire the property till later in the century by gift from Fulk Paynel. Uffculme church must be far older. If there was not already a church there, the monks of Glastonbury would have built one when they first acquired Uffculme in the middle of the ninth century. The dedication in honour of St Mary makes this likely as the Old Church of St Mary was the most revered shrine at Glastonbury. The church was later given to the Priory of Bath (Bath Abbey), to which it belonged throughout the Middle Ages, though the lay lords of the manor occasionally disputed the right of presentation.

The Old Parsonage

The Old Parsonage, now a private residence, has remains of a modest dwelling house of the fourteenth century. It was probably the residence of the medieval Rectors appointed by Bath. In 1302, the church of Uffculme was said to hold a half of Yondercott. The house was rebuilt and provided with better rooms in about 1600, when the presentation and possession of the church had passed to Salisbury and the incumbent of Uffculme became only a Vicar with Salisbury holding the Rectory and most of the money. There is still a prebend of Uffculme at Salisbury, though the estates have passed to the Ecclesiastical Commissioners and the presentation to the Diocese of Exeter.

The Church Building

The parish church of St Mary the Virgin consists of nave and chancel, north aisle and two south aisles, with a western tower and steeple and north and south porches. The oldest part of the present building is the western part of the north arcade. Three pointed arches, each of two chamfered members, rise from circular columns with chamfered bases and moulded capitals. These arches date from the thirteenth century. The original church to which they belonged was typical of the more important parish churches of the time. It had an aisled nave of four bays, with narrow aisles covered by pent roofs, and a small chancel, probably covering the space between the screen and the present chancel arch. The aisles were comparatively low with ranges of small windows above the pent roofs to light the nave. It is likely that a tower was added during the thirteenth or fourteenth century.

Before 1450, the aisles were widened and extended east to flank the chancel. The north aisle with its rubble masonry and large traceried windows survives from this date, though it has been extensively repaired. The south aisle was similar, covering approximately the same area as the present *inner* aisle on that side. The new aisles were the same height as the nave and the church was roofed with three parallel gables. It is clear that the intention was to rebuild the nave arcades. That on the south side was completed in the new Perpendicular style. The north arcade was begun, but stopped one bay west of the screen, where the new arch can be seen on the east side rising from the older column. Money probably ran out, but the completion of the eastern part was necessary to accommodate the screen, which is contemporary with this rebuilding. As Uffculme was a large parish, the chancel was probably lengthened at the same time.

The rood screen is a fine and early example of the typical Devon form with fan vaulting carrying the rood loft, of which only the floor remains; the parapets have been removed together with the

Walrond tomb and busts, St Mary's Church.
(Photo C Stokes)

figures for which the screen was designed. The present cross is modern. Access to the rood loft was by a stair turret in the north wall, which still remains.

The responsibility for the chancel fell upon the Rector or the patrons and neither may have felt it necessary to incur the expense. Monastic patrons, like Bath Abbey, were often loth to spend money. In 1452 the Bishop of Exeter found it necessary to set up a commission to enquire into the dilapidations of the rectory and the chancel and the defects in the service books and to sequester the goods of the lately-vacated Rector, John Haydore. Any rebuilding or extension of the chancel must have taken place after this date. The north porch is an addition to the aisle, possibly as much as fifty years later. It has a room over the porch for storing the parish chest and other documents. The big change dates from the middle of the nineteenth century when the chancel was entirely rebuilt. A fuller account of the Victorian restorations is given in the contribution by Dr C Brooks on page 48.

The Walrond Chapel at the east end of the north aisle, beyond the screen was refitted in about 1950. The panelling on the east wall came from Bradfield, but the altar and reredos are modern with ancient panels inserted. Under the north window is a large altar tomb. The inscription and the arms show that it was erected in 1663 as a tomb for William Walrond (died 1667) and his wife Ursula Speccot (died 1698). Their portraits appear in low relief medallions on the front of the tomb. Three busts rest on the tomb itself. They are in costume of the earlier seventeenth century. The man and woman probably represent Henry Walrond and Penelope Sidnam, the parents of William Walrond. Henry died in 1650 and it is probable that the tomb was erected by William both as a memorial to his parents and for his own burial and that of his wife. The boy probably represents Henry, the fourth son of Henry and Penelope. The younger Henry died in 1638. The recumbent figure in armour is probably Sir William Walrond, the elder son of William and Ursula. He died a bachelor in 1689 and the property passed to his younger brother.

The modern tower screen incorporates panels from the Jacobean western gallery which was demolished about 1925. The pulpit bears the date 1719 and the names Francis Webb and Nicholas Tucker, churchwardens in that year. The font is a part of the nineteenth century restoration in the Gothic style. The Royal Arms have been reset above the tower arch.

Bradfield

The Walronds obtained the estate at Bradfield in the twelfth century by a grant from Fulk Paynel. In 1332, John Walrond obtained a licence to have mass celebrated in his chapel at Bradfield, the rights of the parish church at Uffculme being reserved. The oldest part of the present house is the great hall facing east. It has an original hammer-beam roof of four bays. The porch and the screens passage were at the south end, with the service wing beyond. Most of the other detail, including the reset panelling is later. The hall dates from the second half of the fifteenth century. The north wing, which contained the private apartments, was entirely rebuilt in the late sixteenth century when new windows were inserted in the hall. The rooms on the ground floor of the north wing have fine Jacobean panelling and rich plaster ceilings. A fuller account is given on page 42.

Walrond Chapel. Modern altar with ancient panels inserted.
(Photo G H Hall)

A VICAR REFLECTS: THE REV'D JAMES WINDSOR (1783-1833)

by Adrian Reed

IN 1799 the Rev'd Windsor made his first entry in a large manuscript volume to which he was to turn at infrequent intervals over the next quarter century to record matters he considered noteworthy. Unfortunately he was not a diarist and his choice of events, with sometimes a decade between them, was highly selective. More valuable is the attempt he made in 1810 to assess the changes in the life of Uffculme over the preceding century. His first pages were penned in considerable irritation.

Although, in 1799, the likelihood of a French invasion was no greater than in earlier years, the Government issued instructions to all villages within twenty miles of the coast, which included Uffculme, as to the action to be taken should the French land. These provided for the destruction of stocks of food and fodder and for the evacuation of able-bodied men with animals and transport to either Dartmoor or Sedgemoor, as geographically appropriate. Responsibility for carrying out these orders in the parishes rested with the incumbents who, with their churchwardens, were to remain behind to ensure that all ricks and other stores were fired. Windsor's main criticism was that once on Sedgemoor there would be nothing for man or beast to eat!

Uffculme in 1799

The Government also required a report on the state of each parish and that of the Rev'd Windsor gives an interesting account of Uffculme's human and agricultural resources at the time. The total population in the year 1799 was also, appropriately, 1799, of which 407 were able-bodied men between the ages of 15 and 60. A further 80 in that age group were unfit for active service, 9 were away with the Volunteers and 13 were Quakers. Of the remainder, all judged incapable of removing themselves, 761 were women and children, while 529 were described as being infirm or infants. Livestock included 1838 sheep, 585 cows, 439 pigs, 531 young cattle and colts and 78 oxen. There were 154 draught and 35 saddle horses with 74 carts and 21 waggons. Amongst the dead stock held were 450 loads of hay, 1060 bags of potatoes, 420 quarters of wheat, 178 of oats, 252 of barley and 115 of malt. There were two cornmills in the parish with a combined grinding capacity of 300 bushels a week while the 127 recorded bread ovens could bake 788 bushels in 24 hours.

From these figures come the picture of an agricultural pattern not greatly different from to-day's, with the pastoral element predominant. Oxen were still used for ploughing and much of the cereal production was for domestic consumption by man and beast. The malt stocks reflect the wide extent of domestic brewing as do the numerous ovens that of home bread making. Surprising, perhaps, is the comparatively small number of saddle horses, taking into account that most of the land-owning gentry would have more than one animal in their stables. The reason may lie in the demands of the army—and the prices paid. Another question mark must be put against the 39 packs of flax in the list. Were they grown here and where were they sold?

Jubilee of George III

When next the Rev'd Windsor took up his pen it was to record the events of the 'Day of Jubilee or public Rejoicing' to mark the beginning of the fiftieth year of the reign of King George III on 25 October 1809. The high point of the celebrations was the planting 'in the Presence of a vast Concourse of People' of two horse chestnut trees in the churchyard, 'the nuts thereof brought by Richard Hall Clarke Esq of Bridwell from His Majesty's garden at Richmond', under the superintendence of the donor and the Vicar, to the accompaniment of the National Anthem. In spite of this auspicious start the tree nearest the church tower lost its top within a few days. Mr Clarke provided a replacement which suffered the same fate. Undeterred in his fight against vandalism the Vicar obtained from Exeter a larger tree of the same species which seems to have proved more durable. The second of the two royal trees lasted until December 1810 when it, too, was broken down. Once again the Vicar procured an older and stouter substitute from Exeter.

Coronation of George IV

A decade later the Rev'd Windsor copied into his book a newspaper report of the celebration of the Coronation of George IV in 1821. All houses in the villages were decorated with greenery and there were numerous triumphal arches. The bells began pealing in the early morning and at ten o'clock all those forming part of the great procession were given a breakfast of bread, cheese and cider.

Lead by a troop of Yeomanry Cavalry it moved off to the accompaniment of two bands, members of the various Clubs falling in behind their banners. All were said to have marched in excellent order to Gaddon Down where they were given more cider. What they did there besides drinking is not recorded but by two o'clock they were back in the village with their numbers now brought up to about 1500 by the women and children who joined them there. In the centre they found seats for all at a dinner of brown bread, beef and cider 'of the very best quality'. At four o'clock it was the turn of the village gentry, nearly thirty of whom sat down to a dinner at the Fountain Tavern 'served up in Hellier's (the landlord's) best style' and drank 'many loyal toasts with rapturous applause and Mirth'. Afterwards they all, one hopes, were in a condition to accompany their wives and daughters to the Ball in the Schoolroom 'tastefully decorated for the occasion' and firmly under the control of the Rev'd V E Manley 'who conducted it with the greatest Order and Decorum' until two o'clock the following morning.

To finance these junketings £81-6s-0d had been raised by public subscription to which had to be added the value of five hogsheads of cider worth £12 that were given free. The Rev'd Windsor noted with satisfaction that a balance of £13-17s-9d remained to be banked in Tiverton for distribution to the poor of the village the following winter. Cider consumption must have averaged pretty near half-a-gallon a head for every man, woman and child in the village. Two generations later celebrants of Queen Victoria's 1887 Jubilee are reported to have drunk 120 gallons of tea!

A century of change recorded

In 1810 the Rev'd Windsor set down his reflections on changes in the life of the parish over the previous ninety years, changes that he considered to be greater than in preceding centuries. Uffculme had the advantage of numerous streams, so from early days, it had prospered with the wool trade. The increase in wealth and population was marked by the two galleries added to the church in 1631 and the third some ninety years later. This happy state reached its peak in about 1745, thereafter 'regularly decreasing'. He regretted the passing of the days when 'men but of small capital, which, if they were industrious they had an opportunity of rapidly increasing' while 'all females belonging to labourers of every Description' worked at a spinning wheel. Now there was not a comber or weaver under thirty five, none having been trained in the previous twenty years. In fact, the Parish was paying £30 a year to a Mr Upcott of Cullompton 'on condition of his finding employment in the woollen trade for such as were formerly bred to it'.

This widespread unemployment in the woollen industry was in his view caused by the introduction of water-driven machinery. The result was that clothiers 'whose capital consisted of but a few hundred pounds, who though not rich, were independent and happy, were now suddenly reduced to Poverty as they could not render their Goods sufficiently (cheap) to ensure a sale, and afford them any Profit'. A most melancholy scene ensued with men in their old age forced to take any job to avoid starvation. Families were broken up and the children sent away because there were far more than the local farmers could take as apprentices. The first mill in the Parish, that at Bradfield, started around 1795 and the Coldharbour Mill a little later. Bradfield closed down in the eighteen sixties and Coldharbour was turned into a Working Wool Museum in 1982.

Mills had 'sprung up all over the country, every man who wished suddenly to be rich having recourse to them but Bankruptcies were too frequently the Consequences'. Yet there was an even darker side to these new enterprises than the unemployment they caused. Once one was set up 'A General Depravity of Manners and an horrid Indecency in Words and Gestures particularly among the females immediately ensued, far worse than what is to be met within the Streets of the largest Cities in the Kingdom, together with an insatiable Appetite for Show and Finery in Dress wholly unsuited to their Situation in Life, and they may properly be termed the Seedbeds in which Filth, Vermin and Vice germinate, and the Hotbeds which maintain them'. But, then, the highly principled Mr Fox who founded Coldharbour Mill was a Quaker and as such may not have had the merits of his establishment acknowledged!

Nevertheless, the *pre*-mill days of the Uffculme woollen industry were not altogether idyllic. While the 'females belonging to labourers' were busily spinning away, their menfolk, if woolcombers or weavers, might well have been engaged in terrorising the local shop- and inn-keepers. If any of these traders were accused of 'unfair practices they were levied a fine at their Discretion and if they did not pay they and their families were prohibited all further dealings with them until they did so.' The fines, of course, were spent on liquor. Not even their employers escaped their insolence, sometimes being dragged by force to their Clubhouse. This went on until one William Hucker, who had had earlier brushes with the mob, had them indicted at Exeter where they were severely punished. Before this baker's courageous action the 'Inhabitants stood in awe of them as their numbers rendered them truly formidable'. The tyranny exercised by these 'Clubs', and their downfall, was in the decade 1760-1770 according to the Rev'd Windsor's information. Earlier their affairs had been conducted in an even more boisterous manner.

The Culmstock riot

Sometime between 1720 and 1730, 'according to the unanimous Tradition of Old Men', the Societies (probably both of weavers and combers) of Cullompton, Bradninch, Silverton and Thorverton assembled together in a body and marched to Culmstock 'in Consequence of a dispute between them and their Brethren of Uffculme, Culmstock and Hemyock, all armed with such weapons as Rage or Chance supplied'. The husbandmen of Uffculme came out in support of their up-valley neighbours, brandishing their flails and a general engagement took place in the streets of Culmstock. 'Limbs were broken and at last the Assailants were routed after leaving many of their Company behind who were confined as Prisoners in the Tower'.

At least one unfortunate was 'hewn asunder by a scythe fixed on a pole': other fatalities were not recollected by the 'Old Men'. The magistrates sent the prisoners under military escort to Exeter gaol where, in due course, 'they suffered that punishment which the Law invariably inflicts on those who seek a Redress of Grievances by Riot and Tumult'. Though deplorable, the Culmstock affair was by no means unique, the protests of Devon woollen workers during the reigns of the first two Georges ending, as often as not, in general riots.

Some general improvements

In spite of the distress in the woollen industry, the Rev'd Windsor found improvements to record. Tea drinking was no longer a pleasure of the rich—an efficient smuggling system ensured that, many houses had carpets and the umbrella provided universal protection. Most important, both in itself and in its consequence, was the improvement in communications. Before the coming of the turnpike roads in the seventeen fifties, movement by wheeled vehicle was virtually impossible. The gentry who tried, sent their footmen ahead to clear obstacles. MPs going to London needed a yoke of oxen to help their horses up Honiton Hill. Most things were moved by pack horses to whose saddles were fixed crooks with lengths varied according to the goods to be transported—long for hay, short for small barrels of liquor. Dung was carried in pots with a removable peg securing the bottom. Heavy barrels were loaded on drays, other bulky items were dragged on slides.

With the turnpikes came an improvement in lesser roads. Surveyors of the Highways were authorised to take money instead of labour from parishes. Before this 'labour days' tended to be drunken affairs. Payment now could be in cash and not in liquor, to the general improvement of the road system. But the main effect of the new turnpikes, in the Rev'd Windsor's view, was the benefit they conferred on agriculture. At about the time they were built, the practice started of making butter by the churn. This made for quicker production and with the new highways it became possible to send casks of salted butter to London. This was so profitable that farmers turned from tillage to pasture. The rent of grazing land trebled in consequence.

The Rev'd Windsor's incumbency began in the year which saw the end of the American Revolutionary War and concluded in that following the passing of the Great Reform Bill. Apart from his initial outburst against the Government's evacuation policy and the transcription of a press report of Napoleon's retreat from Moscow, outside events find no place in his writings. Neither did they in those of Jane Austin. What we *do* get from him is the frank, if prejudiced, views of a country parson about the industrial changes and their social consequences which he did not fully understand and could only fear. There must have been many others like him in England at the time.

NICHOLAS AYSHFORD'S GIFT TO UFFCULME
by Elaine Seale

IN 1793 Richard Hall Clarke Esq. of Bridwell and others began to make enquiries, and officials in Chancery began to ask questions. George Greenway, the schoolmaster of Ayshford School, Uffculme, had died in 1789 being owed 18 years' salary.

The facts seem to be that Nicholas Ayshford, Gentleman, of Taunton St Mary, left Robert Kerslake £1,200 on trust, to build a school and schoolhouse in Uffculme and use the rest of the money to purchase lands 'for endowing the same'. Robert Kerslake *did* build the school and schoolhouse at a cost of £400. But he kept the remaining £800 'in his hands till his death' in 1722. He was mortgagee (for more than their value) of two houses in South Street, Wellington, which he left to his two sons in trust to use the rents towards repairing the 'free school at Uffculme' and, reciting that he had the above-mentioned £800 in his hands, he directed his executor to make a purchase therewith of land-in-fee, and settle the same on trustees for the payment of the schoolmaster for the time being and if there was need, use some of the money to repair the school and schoolhouse.

When the two sons died the 'estate' was left to another Robert Kerslake, the grandson, and he paid the then schoolmaster until 1769 but the schoolhouse was not repaired. When the grandson died in 1771 the estate passed to his brothers-in-law Thomas and Cornelius Marsh.

It would seem that George Greenway was appointed in 1771 but he received no salary for this services. He died in 1789 and ten years later his representatives finally received £646 18s 4d.

Not until 1802 was a scheme put forward and confirmed by the Court of Chancery appointing 'Twelve principal inhabitants of the parish and neighbourhood of Uffculme' as trustees. They were required to appoint a Treasurer and 'settle accounts and transact affairs of the charity . . .' and 'elect a proper person, being a graduate of one of the Universities, in holy orders and of adequate learning, to be master of the free school of Uffculme . . . with the approbation of the Dean of Sarum . . .'. A fund was set up, repairs to the school and schoolhouse were put in hand, and the Rev'd Edward Manley was elected schoolmaster, commencing from midsummer 1803.

The school was to be '. . . at all times free for tuition, gratis, to four boys to be chosen by the trustees, of which boys, two were to be of the parish of Uffculme, and two of the parishes of Burlescombe and Holcombe Rogus'. The education was to be a classical one and the boys were also taught English and writing '... without any expense, except the charge of a few shillings for books, although the master did not feel himself bound to give them instruction in the two last-mentioned branches'. The arrangement did not flourish. In October 1907, it was reported that since 1803 only five boys had been appointed by the trustees, three from Uffculme, one from Burlescombe and one from Holcombe Rogus. The reason for the dis-interest was that the inhabitants were 'not desirous of obtaining a classical education for their sons'.

In 1872, a scheme to establish a day school exclusively for girls was put forward, but it did not prove satisfactory. Later, in April 1879, the governors were authorised to lease the school to the Devon and Somerset County Girls' School Association. The building was to be used 'for the purpose of . . . providing education for girls of a higher grade than that afforded in public elementary schools'. But this scheme never came into operation and no rent was paid.

(from a watercolour by Peter Orlando Hutchinson) (Devon County Record Office)

In 1887, yet another scheme evolved whereby the school was to be a day and boarding school for boys, suited to prepare the scholars for 'afterwards pursuing their education at Blundell's

School at Tiverton and other like schools'. This scheme seems to have been in operation for some 22 years. A report published by the Charity Commissioners in 1909 gives the number of boys as 17, of whom 11 were boarders. Their report goes on to say, '. . . Blundell's School now has a preparatory school connected with it in Tiverton; but it is thought that the Ayshford School will continue to be useful and may increase.'.

A pupil who attended the school between 1917-1921 remembers Mr Prideau and Mr Bertram Mould as headmasters, and Miss Barrows (whose brother was Mayor of Tiverton) as one of the teachers. When she left, Miss Lena F Martin (who died in 1983) was appointed. The Curate, Mr Prowse taught latin at that time. The Rev'd Hubert G Chalk of Kentisbeare wrote a school song, which hopefully improved in the singing:

Fair set in creamy Devonshire   And I'll ne'er forget thee now
Amid the level Blackdowns   I've worn the Ash Keys
An ancient school I spy.   I've worn the Ash Keys
I'm one of Ayshford   The Ash Keys on my brow.
I'm one of Ayshford

The Minutes of the first meeting of the Trustees of the Ayshford Educational Foundation are dated February 1st 1923 and it seems that the formation of this trust marked the end of Ayshford Grammar School as such. The minutes speak of prize cups and a hand-bell being in the keeping of Mr Clarke and of a resolution to pass these to the home.

Local people tell stories of the school buildings being used as an orphanage and children from 'Ayshford House', Shillingford, being brought to live in it. They were kept apart from the village children, wore uniform and went to chuch in a 'crocodile'.

A conveyance dated 10th March 1955 marked the end of the building as a school. It states '. . . that in consideration of £2,000 paid by the Rural District Council of Tiverton to the County Council of the Administrative County of Devon, the said County Council conveys unto the Rural Council ALL THAT property known as Ayshford Children's Home formerly known as 'The Ayshford School' . . .'.

The property is now used as local authority housing, but its original purpose is still clearly evident in its architectural features.

UFFCULME DURING THE EARLY VICTORIAN YEARS
by Pat Regardsoe

THE opening of the long reign of Queen Victoria in 1837 seemed to pass by the village of Uffculme. There is no direct mention of it in any parish records. This is perhaps surprising to us in retrospect but, at the time, the accession of a young German princess probably seemed of little importance compared to the changes taking place in the parish itself.

This was a period of change nationally as the industrial revolution gradually altered the economic balance of the country from agriculture to industry. Uffculme had already seen the virtual destruction of the cottage textile industry with the building of the mills at Coldharbour and Bradfield. The changes also affected agriculture, with the building of the turnpike road (now the A38 and B3181) linking the Culm Valley with the rest of Devon and England. The Rev'd Windsor describes how these changes affected Uffculme in the late eighteenth and early nineteenth centuries, see page 15.

By 1850 the Great Western Railway, engineered by Isambard Kingdom Brunel, had been extended from Bristol to Plymouth. Although it was not until 1876 that the Culm Valley Light Railway opened it was still possible for people from Uffculme to reach stations at Cullompton or Burlescombe and to travel or send goods to all parts of England quickly and cheaply.

The period we are looking at is one where some changes had already taken place but where there is still evidence of the self-sufficient community that had grown up in the valley over previous centuries.

White's Directory of 1850 describes Uffculme as a 'decayed market town'. Certainly the prosperity of the cottage workers was by then a thing of the past. There had been a regular weekly market, the grant for which was given in 1266, but this had declined and was by then 'nearly obsolete'. There were still, however, three annual fairs held on the Wednesday after Good Friday, June 29th and the second Wednesday in September. These were no doubt enjoyed by the people of the whole parish not just by those who lived in the town of Uffculme itself.

Uffculme then, as now, was not only a small town, but a parish. Many of the appropriate documents relate to the parish, the boundaries of which were very important demarcation lines that were annually beaten to ensure that there was no encroachment by the neighbouring parishes of Culmstock, Burlescombe, Halberton,

Willand, Kentisbeare, Sheldon or Hemyock. Despite the proximity of these parishes there was little liaison between them. This is borne out by the parish registers. Between January 1837 and December 1844 there were 144 banns of marriage called. Of all the 288 individuals involved only one man and two women came from Culmstock, one man and one woman from Halberton, one man from Bishops Hull, one woman from Cullompton and another from Broadhembury. Apart from these eight people, all the others came from within the parish of Uffculme. Many of the names on these lists are still familar within the parish and surrounding areas today. Some examples are Moon, Cottrell, Perry, Wyatt, Doble, Clist, Veals, Blackmoor, Maunder, Eveleigh, Middleton and Broom.

The effects of enclosure

Except on the boundaries between Culmstock and Willand, the adjoining parishes along the Culm Valley, Uffculme is surrounded by higher land. Towards the head of the valley there were many ancient barrows which were commemorated in the field names. Until the beginning of the nineteenth century these higher areas were open common land, much as Culmstock Beacon is today. This land was used by members of the parish to graze animals and for turf, furze and wood for fuel. When they were too overcrowded, they were allowed to build a house on this land and reside in it as long as there was smoke coming out of the chimney within twenty-four hours of the start of building. Building was often done on midsummer's day. These people then became 'squatters'.

Between 1795 and 1815 the Napoleonic wars stopped grain being imported. This, coupled with extremely bad harvests, meant that the price of corn shot up. There was an incentive to bring as much land as possible into grain production hoping to cash in on these high prices. As a result there was, throughout the country, a move to enclose common land which could then be used in this way. Numerous Acts of Parliament authorising these 'inclosures' (to use the old spelling) were passed. Uffculme came in rather late on this idea and the royal assent to enclosure was not given until 12th May 1815.

Altogether 480 acres were allowed to be enclosed at Gaddon Down, Uffculme Down, Smithincott Green, Hackpen Hill, Northcott Pitt and Moor, Ashill and Rull Green. The enclosure of these areas of common land meant that people who had traditional rights lost them, but in compensation they were given a proportion of the land according to their stated rights. Large landowners, like the Lord of the Manor of Uffculme, William Hurley, and the Lord of the Manor of Hackpen, Charles Leigh gained most out of the enclosure. Both laid claim to the soil and the trees on these common lands, so obviously they expected the largest areas to be allocated to them. An impartial commissioner, Joseph Easton from Somerset, was in charge of this reallocation of land.

Of the 480 acres, forty were set aside for the poor people of the parish to cut turves etc and five acres became gravel and stone pits to provide surfacing material for new roads within the parish.

By 1837, these enclosures had been completed and absorbed into the landholdings of those with the required rights, most of whom were the richer residents of the parish who paid poor rate. The areas of enclosed land are quite clear on a map of the parish today because of their straight roads and square or rectangular field patterns.

With the ending of the Napoleonic wars the original incentive for enclosing the land disappeared. There was also a miraculous improvement in the weather producing, nationally, a glut of grain and drastically reducing its price. An agricultural depression followed when many farmers could not afford to keep going and even less, to improve their holding. The two major landowners who were allocated much of the enclosed land solved their problems in different ways.

By 1841 Richard Hurley was eighty years old. He was not only the Lord of the Manor but also a surgeon and he lived at Gaddon House. He owned a total of 590 acres of which he farmed 245 himself. Most of the land that he farmed he had put into plantations presumably to cash in on the need for wood rather than corn. This eighty-year-old gentleman must have been rather lonely. It appears that he had no family living with him, only two female students and two young agricultural labourers. It is, however, possible that Martha Hurley, 75, who was staying at the vicarage on the night of the 1841 census was either his wife or an unmarried sister.

By 1841 Charles Leigh was no longer mentioned and so had presumably died. Two members of the Leigh family were landowners, Mary who owned 70 acres and Edward Manley who owned 214 acres. All of Mary's land, Park, was let to John Pring. Edward Manley let most of his land to Edward White and John Tancock, only farming a small plantation of 25 acres himself. Neither of these members of the Leigh family lived within the parish and, in fact, Leigh Barton was then owned by William Ayshford Wood, aged thirty. He had a wife, two young children and five servants living in the house. He farmed 440 acres of the land around Leigh Barton, presumably with the help of agricultural labourers who lived in the vicinity.

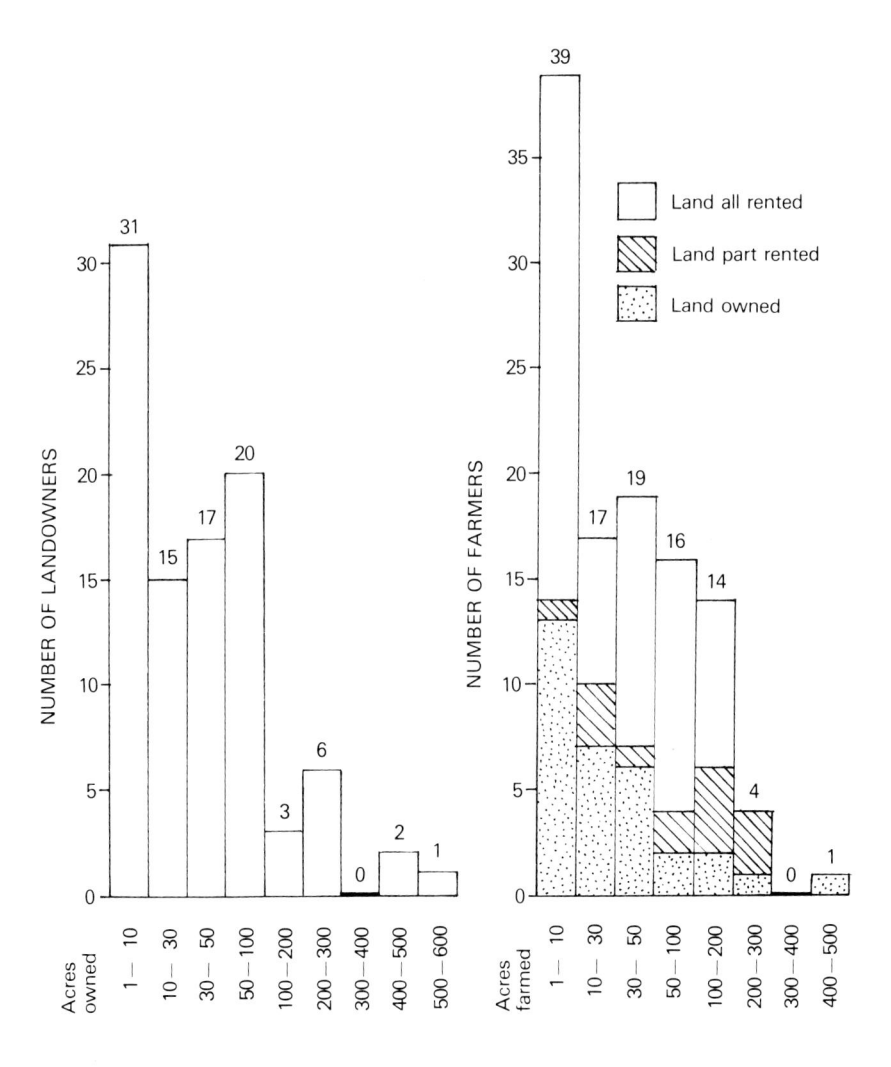

Fig 1 Landowners.

Fig 2 Farmers.

Land ownership and use

The land of the parish had a number of major uses. By far the largest areas were designated 'arable' although this does not denote what type of crop was planted or whether or not it was rotated with grass in the form of leys. Along the edges of streams and the Culm itself, there was meadow land with scattered areas of pasture close by. Plantations were mostly on higher land towards Blackborough, Gaddon and Hillhead, although many other high areas were arable. Orchards were to be found around all farms and hamlets, but there were larger concentrations around Ashill, Smithincott, Yondercott and Craddock. Some of the enclosed land near Hackpen was obviously not productive and was designated as 'furze' or 'brake' and a few areas both here and near Five Fords on the boundary with Culmstock had not been fenced. Most of the land was, however, apparently in productive use.

Figure 1 shows the number of landowners for different acreages within the parish. Figure 2 shows the number of farmers (some of whom owned all or part of the land that they farmed) for different acreages. If we take the twelve largest areas of land in the parish, we find definite differences as shown in figures 1 and 2. Of the twelve landowners of 100 acres or more five were absentee landlords who actually *farmed* little or no land within the parish. Conversely there were two farmers in the twelve largest who owned *no* land and two others who owned no land but who farmed over 100 acres. Not surprisingly, all these farmers did live in the parish.

Henry Doble in 1841 owned and/or farmed much of the same land that his descendant Edward Doble does today.

Name	Age	Location	Acres owned	Acres farmed	Lived in parish
Richard Hurley	80	Gaddon	590	245	Yes
William Ayshford Wood	30	Leigh	470	440	Yes
William Walrond	80	Bradfield	427	36	Yes
John New, Dr of Physics	71	Craddock	240	0	Yes
John New, Jnr	40	Craddock	90	274	Yes
Richard Marker		Scattered	257	22	No
Penny Whitter / Frances Southwood		Stennal	238	8	No
Corporation of Exeter		Foxhill	232	0	No
Edward Manley Leigh		Hackpen	214	25	No
Sarah Cornish		Southill	208	0	No
John Garnsey	35	Bodmiscombe	176	176	Yes
Frances Broom, Jnr	45	Sheldon	174	174	Yes
Clement Venn	55	Northcott	159	163	Yes

Fig. 3 Large landowners

The landowners listed opposite owned a total of 3481 acres of land, ie just over half of the parish total of 6123 acres. The remainder was owned by many people, some of whom were substantial farmers.

The ownership of the rest of the land was divided up as follows:

    31 people owned between 1 and 10 acres
    15 people owned between 10 and 30 acres
    17 people owned between 30 and 50 acres
    20 people owned between 50 and 100 acres

Land was obviously not the only property. Many other people owned houses, cottages, workshops and so on that they used themselves or rented to others.

Name	Age	Location	Acres owned	Acres farmed
William Ayshford Wood	30	Leigh	472	440
John New, Jnr	40	Craddock	93	274
Henry Doble	50	Parsonage	66	261
Richard Hurley	80	Gaddon	590	245
Thomas Pring (two names possibly father and son)	62 / 20	Ashill & Smithincott	33	223
John Garnsey	35	Bodmiscombe	176	176
Frances J Broom	45	Sheldon	174	174
Clement Venn	55	Northcott	159	163
William Wood	66	Rull	76	160
Frances Trott	50	Brook	19	157
Edward White	60	Hackpen	0	143
John Trott	50	Foxhill	0	120
William Trott	30	Southill	0	106
William Hewett	40	Osmonds	0	101

Fig 4: Large farmers

As can be seen from figure 4, the age of the farmers who worked the land was on average, lower than that of the landowners. These fourteen farmers worked a total of 2743 acres which indicates that for farming, the land was divided into smaller units. This is not surprising in the days before mechanisation. The sixty two farmers in the parish were aided by 164 farm labourers and eleven apprentice farmers.

Many of those who farmed did so in small units. As may be seen from figure 2, thirty nine used land areas between one and ten acres. You could, in those days, call yourself 'a farmer' if you owned and farmed twenty two acres, as did John Knight at Batts. It was, however, not only farmers who owned land. It may seem surprising that Sarah Mills, a fifty-five-year-old pauper should own land, but this was so. She owned one-and-a-half acres at Ashill and lived there with four children between the ages of seven and fifteen. They bore her surname and would probably have been grandchildren. Some agricultural labourers also farmed land. Lewis Parish rented one-and-a-quarter acres presumably to help supplement his income. He was not alone. There were seven other agricultural labourers as well as five carpenters who either owned or rented land. Land was also owned by masons, millers and blacksmiths. So land ownership was not only in the hands of the richer members of the parish although they did have the lion's share.

Occupations

Figure 5 shows the occupations of residents in the parish of Uffculme, as listed in the census return of 1841. The census shows the people who slept at a particular residence on the night of 9th June 1841. It does not state the relationships within each household or absentees who normally lived there. Assumptions can be made, but it should be borne in mind that that is exactly what they are. The other factor relating to the 1841 census is that it usually states the occupation of the principal 'breadwinner' of the household and ignores the other members. The 1851 census, in comparison, is much more detailed even showing 'scholars'. The 1841 census has been used, however, because it most nearly fits the time when the tythe apportionment document was published; 1839 in the case of Uffculme. Even so, an analysis is still very useful, enabling us to see what many of the people of the parish did and it does give a picture of the occupational structure. The three largest occupational groups were servants (184), agricultural labourers (164) and labourers in the woollen factories (106). These figures merit individual study.

Servants can be considered 'non-productive'. They worked mostly in the homes of the larger farmers and people of independent means, another large 'occupational' group (59).

It is interesting to study the ages of these servants. Figure 6 shows that the majority were in the age range ten to twenty years and in the case of male servants there was only one over the age of forty. If this is compared to the ages of agricultural labourers it can be postulated that once boys became strong enough, most of them moved from the farmhouses to the fields. The life of an agricultural labourer must have been a reasonably healthy one, despite the hard work and damp living conditions, as many were still active well after today's retirement age.

Female servants also tended to be young, but the reason is probably different. Most girls who went into service lived in and as soon as they married this was no longer possible so that they were forced to give up their jobs.

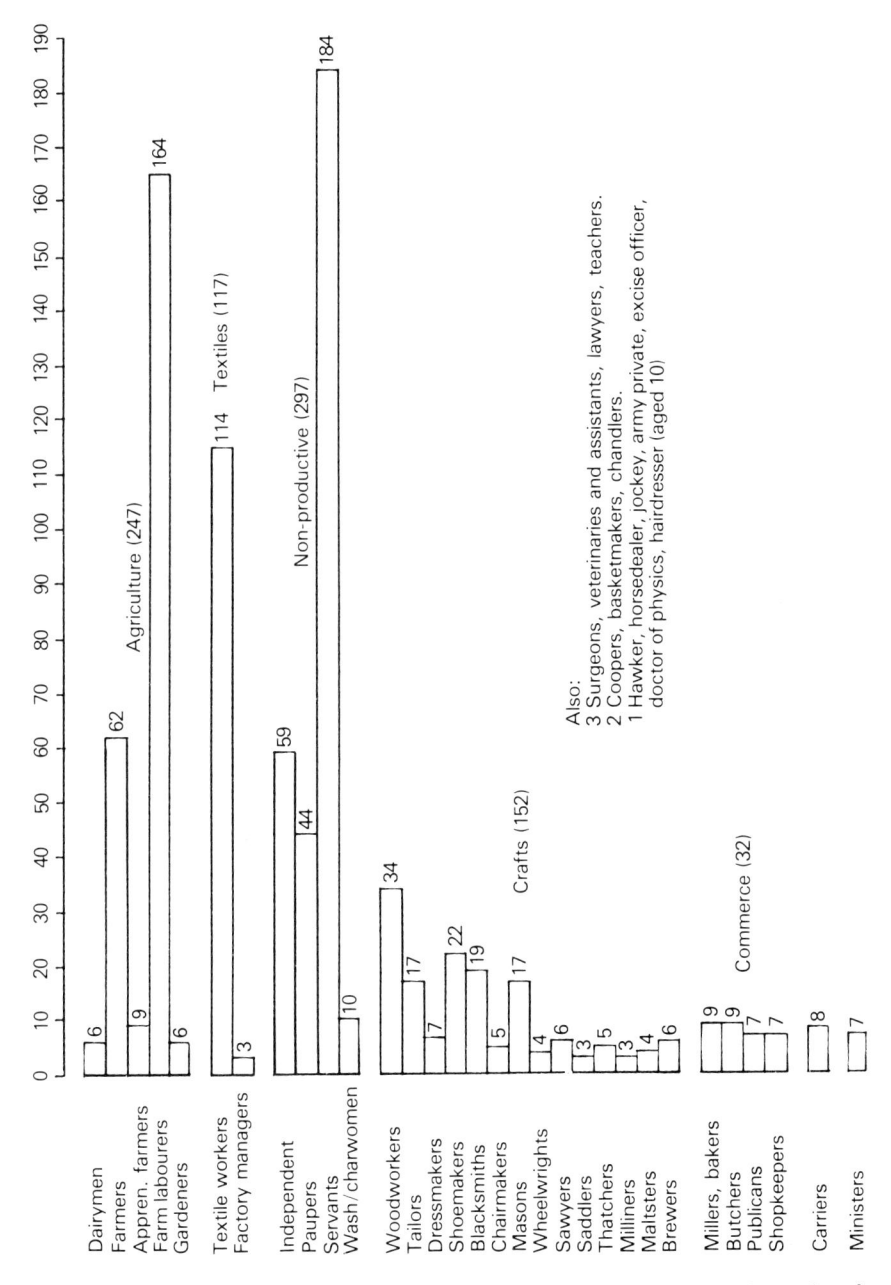

Fig. 5 *Occupations of those resident in the parish of Uffculme on the night of 7 June 1841.*

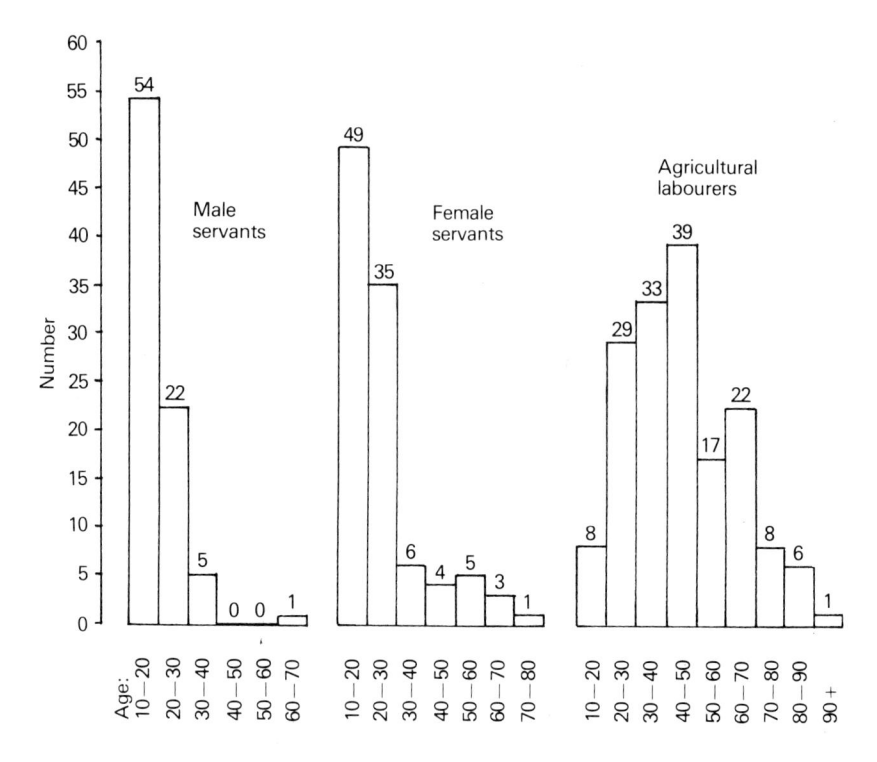

Fig. 6 Ages of some major occupational groups in Uffculme, 7 June 1841.

There were at that time two textile mills in the parish of Uffculme. The major one at Coldharbour, was owned by the Fox family of Wellington and managed by Samuel Sparkes, aged fifty five. He lived at Coldharbour, owning an orchard and three cottages with gardens. He also rented seven acres of land from the Fox family. Coldharbour Mill spun yarn for the Wellington firm and to do this it employed ninety one people, see figure 7, most of whom were young women.

The Bradfield mill was, by comparison, a much smaller affair. It employed only fourteen people who lived in the Bradfield area. The mill was owned by William Walrond of Bradfield House but was let to William Upcott who also had mills at Culmstock and Cullompton. The sale, in 1870, of effects from Upcott's three mills, see figure 8, provide a clue about the uses to which the mills were put. Bradfield mill had all the machinery for the production of woollen and worsted cloth compared to Coldharbour mill that produced yarn to be woven elsewhere.

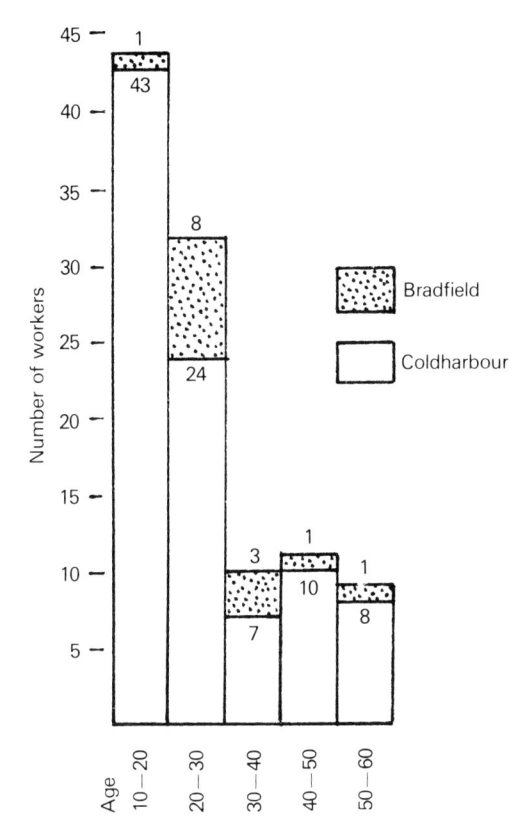

Fig 7 Ages of workers at Bradfield and Coldharbour mills, 7 June 1841.

It can be seen from the equipment listed that the process of cloth production was very mechanised in the parish and it can be assumed that much, if not all, the equipment was in use in 1841. Examples of a number of these machines can be seen today in the Coldharbour Mill Museum.

In the census very few individuals specified particular jobs that they did in the factory or which factory they worked in. As there was another factory at Culmstock there were three distinct possibilities. The Culmstock factory was similar to the Bradfield one. Three of the people who did specify their occupations within a factory probably did work in Culmstock as they lived much nearer there. John Preston was a weaver who lived at Craddock. Mary Clode, also a weaver, and Jenny Baker, a warper, both lived at Pilemoor. They all stated that they worked at their trades within a factory.

DEVONSHIRE.

To Woollen Manufacturers, Machinists, General Dealers, and others.

A CATALOGUE
OF THE VALUABLE
MACHINERY & PLANT,

Of the Woollen Mills at Cullompton, Bradfield near Cullompton, and Culmstock, Devon, comprising :--

SIXTY FIVE-QUARTER LOOMS,
BY HODGSON AND OTHER MAKERS,
MODERN SPINNING FRAMES, *(by Taylor & Wordsworth)*,

Capital Condenser, Scribbling & Carding Engines,

SEVEN SPINNING MULES, *(by Leach & Son, & others)*,

Tenter Hook Willey, Brushing & Teazer Machines, Worsted Reels, Warping Bars, Beaming Machines, &c.,

CAPITAL SET OF IRON STEAM RACKS,
HIGH-PRESSURE STEAM BOILER, WITH STEAM GUAGE, &c.

2000 Ft. of Leather Driving Bands,
(From 9 down to 2 inches wide),

VALUABLE HYDRAULIC AND OTHER IRON PRESSES,
WITH THE PRESS PAPERS AND OTHER APPOINTMENTS,

Iron Fulling Stocks, Broad Gig, and Washers,
150 Broad and Narrow Hand Looms,

500 Ft. of Wrought Iron Shafting,

Wheels, Drums, and Gear Work, old Brass, Iron, and Steel, and numerous other Effects.

The Property of Mr. J. S. UPCOTT, of Cullompton, who is retiring from the Woollen Manufacturing Business,

Which will be Sold by Auction,

By MR. J. GRAHAM FOLEY,
OF TROWBRIDGE, WILTSHIRE,

IN THE FOLLOWING ORDER OF SALE.
On Tuesday, the 28th June, 1870, the Machinery & Effects at Bradfield Mill near Cullompton;
On Wednesday, 29th June, the Machinery and Effects, at Culmstock Mill, near Wellington;
On Thursday, June 30th, the Machinery and Effects, at the Lower Mill, and at the Stores of the Old Workhouse and Premises above, Cullompton.

SALE EACH DAY AT TWELVE O'CLOCK PRECISELY.

The Machinery will be on View on and after the 25th June,

N. B. The nearest Railway Station to the Bradfield & Culmstock Mills is the Tiverton Road Station, of the Bristol and Exeter Railway.

Fig 8 Part of the 16-page catalogue of the sale of machinery and plant of the woollen mills at Cullompton, Bradfield and Culmstock, June 1870.

There were also four girls, Hannah and Ann Marshall and Louisa and Ann Fowler who were spinners at a factory. They lived at Yondercott and Parsonage respectively. It is probable that they worked at Coldharbour and they perhaps considered their jobs to be rather more responsible than the rest of the 'labourers'.

Probably the only person who genuinely continued in the cottage industry tradition was John Radford a sixty-five-year-old woolcomber. Woolcombing was a skilled trade preparing long-stapled wool ready to be spun for the making of smooth *worsted* cloth. In comparison, short-stapled wool was *carded* for *woollen* cloth production.

By 1841 both the combing and carding processes had been mechanised and the carders (who were traditionally the young children of the family) and the combers were becoming redundant. In Culmstock, out of seven woolcombers four were over sixty and there was only one in his forty's. John Radford followed this pattern of a dying trade.

The low number of weavers in the parish of Uffculme is surprising when compared to the neighbouring parish of Culmstock. There, weaving formed the third largest occupational group with seventy two people employed in the craft. Although power looms were used in other parts of the country, it is possible that in the Culm valley weavers were still needed to produce the final cloth. Culmstock might easily have been the parish which the Fox family used as their 'outworker' centre. Without some outside 'organisation', neither low numbers of weavers in Uffculme nor high numbers in Culmstock would make sense.

Although weaving was one of the very few trades not carried out within the parish, most people made their own clothes. For the rich there were milliners, dressmakers and tailors. There also seem to have been an incredible number of shoemakers, twenty two, almost the same number as Culmstock. Maybe this was a 'valley' trade with products sent to markets in Cullompton or Exeter but as it was not possible to make shoes at home and as most people walked rather than rode, shoes probably just wore out quickly and had to be replaced frequently.

Buildings in the parish

There were many different craftsmen to build and repair houses and furniture. Masons were the builders of the day. There were seventeen of them, including three different 'Hart' families. Did the present Hemyock builders originally hail from the parish of Uffculme?

Within the building crafts there were other occupations. Some were traditional workers such as thatchers but there was also a brickmaker, a glazier, and a plumber to show how times were changing.

The old buildings of Uffculme were built of stone and cob with thatched roofs. Early photographs and prints show this. Many of these old buildings would have had shutters rather than expensive glass windows. By 1841, newer buildings were being erected of fashionable brick with glazed windows and a few of the richer residents were obviously getting some form of plumbed water supply rather than relying on the traditional sources of well and stream.

The other forms of liquid refreshment also seem to have been available in plenty. There were a number of maltsters and brewers providing the beer and an even larger number of inns where it was sold. In some cases they were on the same premises. Cider apple orchards provided for home-produced beverages. It used to be considered safer to drink alchohol than water, so perhaps the apparent excess of the substance can be justified!

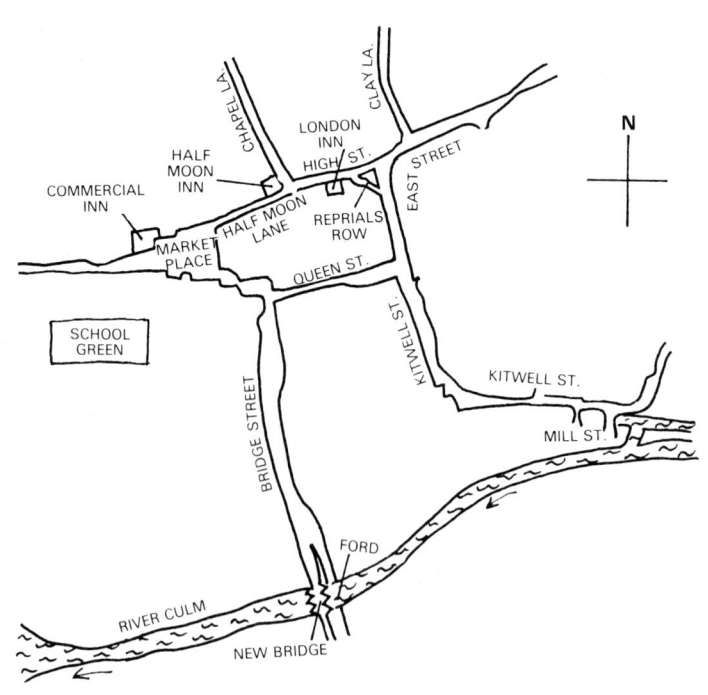

Fig 9 Uffculme street names in 1841.

Uffculme Inns

Half Moon Inn. This was owned by James Holland a wheelwright and let to Ann Banfield. Both were fifty years old. Ann was the publican and she had a daughter aged fifteen.

London Inn. This was also a malthouse and a brewhouse. William Furze (aged sixty) was the brewer, his son John (aged twenty five) worked with him. They also owned one acre of Uffculme Down, enclosed land, and so must originally have had rights on the common, as well as thirteen cottages in the town and Coldharbour. The publican at the London Inn was Richard Damster (aged thirty).

Commercial Inn (now the Ostler). This was owned by Elizabeth Hellier and was rented together with three-and-a-half acres of Uffculme Down by Francis Pratt (aged forty five). He lived at the inn with his wife, daughter and two servants. At this inn there was a skittle garden.

George Inn. This inn, yard, garden and stables were owned by Humphrey Stark. The inn was run by George Tapscott (aged forty) who had a wife and three sons.

Lamb Inn. This seems to have been the most prosperous. It was conveniently placed on the turnpike road and might easily have been a coaching inn. Certainly travellers would have used it and the horsedealer who slept there on the census night was probably one. Benjamin Hussey the landlord (aged sixty five) lived there. There was also a lady of independent means (possibly another traveller), a seventy-year-old maltster, a fifteen-year-old apprentice and four servants.

Benjamin Hussey also owned eighteen-and-a-half acres of land and rented a further fifty eight to make him quite a substantial farmer, although he describes himself only as a publican on the census return.

New Inn. This was at Ashill and was owned and run by William Salter.

In Ashill, William Salter had competition, for opposite him lived John Godfrey who owned a cottage beer house garden and yard. These 'beer houses' existed in other parts of the parish. Presumably they sold beer but did not provide any form of accommodation.

Clergy, gentry and the poor

There were no less than twelve reverend gentlemen who had some connection with the parish. Some owned land, but did not reside within it. The vicar at the time was the Rev'd George Townsend Smith (aged forty) who did not appear to have any family. There were also Baptist, Presbyterian and dissenting ministers and two clerical gentlemen who taught at the Grammar School (Ayshford).

Two distinctly different groups of people did not work for their living. The fifty nine individuals who described themselves as 'independent' had income from the land, industry or inheritance to enable them to live in comfortable idleness. The other group, the forty four paupers, depended on the parish to provide them with sustenance, although there were two paupers with some bread-winners in the family. Sarah Mills was unique in owning property. The majority of both groups were over the age of sixty, thirty one in the case of paupers and thirty six of those of independent means. As far as the paupers were concerned, however, this is probably not an accurate indication of poverty within the parish.

The Poor Law Amendment Act, passed in 1834 stated that no 'able bodied' poor, (ie those who were capable of work), were to be given help either in money or kind in their own homes. This meant that whole dependant families of unemployed 'breadwinners' were forced to go into the workhouse at Tiverton (now Belmont Hospital). As we have already seen, the factory tended to employ young female workers and so did not provide much opportunity to anyone who had lost their jobs in another field.

The parish was a very divided community at the time as was the country as a whole. The rich lived in large houses. They were able to travel and, as servants did most of their work, they had little to do except look after their estates. They were probably unaware of the lives of the poorer members of the community as a whole, even though they would know individuals as workers, fellow churchgoers and so on.

Published in 1982 as the 'Diary of a Devonshire Squire 1844' the journal of John Were Clarke of Bridwell describes some of his life. He travelled to London and Exeter and also to Southampton to see an agricultural show attended by 200,000 people. He was the squire and Lord of the Manor of Halberton but was very involved with Uffculme as his nearest village and because he owned land in the parish. He had a large family of four sons and eight daughters. The fact that so many of his children survived showed that he had concern for their welfare. He mentions in his diary that his son, Thomas, was given a smallpox vaccination and became ill after it, though he survived. A daughter was bought spectacles for £1.13s.0d. No doubt many of the poor 'piecers' in the factory would have benefited from glasses, too, but they would not have been able to afford them.

'John', for example, who was no doubt a servant of Mr Clarke was paid £9 as half-a-year's wages. One can assume that this was the norm for the area and even if some people were paid a little more it would be unlikely that they could afford such luxuries as glasses.

Compared to mill workers in the industrial North of England the workers of Uffculme were well off. The Fox family were considered generous, caring employers. Nearly all the cottages that the workers of whatever trade lived in had gardens in which they could grow their own vegetables. Their life might have been boring, but the large number of working-class people who reached a ripe old age shows that life here was comparatively healthy. The average life expectancy for a working-class person in Manchester at the time was seventeen years. Many of the mill workers gave lodging to others as the long hours worked meant they could not live far away. No doubt their lodging money usefully supplemented family incomes.

Living conditions

House structures in the village and surrounding hamlets have probably not changed much. New buildings have been erected on the fringe of the village but the old houses remain much the same, with the exception of the roofs many of which were once thatched. Inside most houses there have been more obvious changes to make living cleaner, warmer and more comfortable.

There were many fires in the village. In 1844 when there was an exceptionally long drought of twelve weeks there were eleven. Most of these were accidental, caused no doubt by the dry conditions, but at least one resulted from arson. Earlier, in 1826 and 1827, two incidents were reported in the *Exeter Flying Post* when children were burnt to death by their clothes catching on fire. At that time there were no methods of fireproofing clothes and with open fires and cramped living conditions there were obvious dangers.

On 11th August 1842 this entry appeared in the *Exeter Flying Post:*

> 'A serious fire occured on Thursday morning which commenced in the house of Mr Veal, baker and chandler. It was soon discovered and an express was foreworded for the West of England fire engine which soon arrived in the short time of sixteen minutes from Cullompton, followed by the Farmers' engine, in time to prevent greater destruction than the loss of Mr Veal's large premises and three adjoining cottages, all of which were insured in the Imperial Office. No life was lost'.

Business people insured their premises. Obviously the insurance companies co-operated because the 'West of England' insurance company and the 'Farmers' fire engines attended this incident on behalf of 'Imperial'. Other offices mentioned in the *Exeter Flying Post* were the 'Royal Exchange' and the 'Eagle'. Premises so insured had appropriate seals affixed to their fronts.

In 1841 there was no such thing as income tax. Richer residents had to pay tythes to the church and a poor rate which was used to sustain the local paupers and the Tiverton workhouse. They also had to pay a number of other national taxes, most of which would seem strange to us today. Window tax was still being levied and there are some houses in Uffculme today with windows that were obviously blocked up to avoid payment. Some windows in factories, workshops, dairies and, surprisingly, farmhouses were exempt. Others were taxed according to their number and size at approximately ten shillings (50p) per window. There were also taxes on carriages, male servants, horses and dogs and hairpowder. A rather surprising thing was that the tax on individual items *increased* with the number that the person had. For example if someone employed only one male servant he would be charged £1.4s.0d. a year but if he employed two the charge for each was £1.11s.0d. rising to £3.16s.6d. for each additional servant over ten. This was presumably because those employing a number of servants could afford to pay higher taxes but it might appear as an early attempt at redistribution of wealth!

One event that must have excited the interest of all members of the parish is recorded by John Were Clarke in his journal. It was the opening of the railway line from London to Exeter on May 1st 1844. He notes how members of his family went to the Whiteball tunnel to see a train pass. We can assume that they were not alone. From then onwards it was possible to get from Sampford Peverell to London in five hours. A new era was dawning when the villagers of Uffculme would find themselves less isolated and it would not be only the rich who could travel and meet people from other areas. The marriage registers would still show a large number where both parties came from within the parish, but henceforth there would be an increasing number who came from beyond, a thing that would have been unheard of in the early years of Queen Victoria's reign.

Sources

The following material held either at the Devon County Record Office or the West Country Studies Library, Exeter, has been used in compiling this study.

    Parish Registers
    Uffculme tythe apportionment map and document.

Hurleys Lands tythe apportionment map and document.
Census returns 1841.
Diary of a Devonshire Squire 1844, ed. W P Authers.
Enclosure award maps and documents.
Exeter Flying Post.
White's Directory 1850.
Culmstock, a Devon Village.

A copy of the sale catalogue of Cullompton, Bradfield and Culmstock mills is held at Tiverton Museum and part of this is reproduced by kind permission of the Curator.

BRADFIELD
by Dr C A Ralegh Radford

BRADFIELD—the wide open space—lies on the west edge of the Parish of Uffculme. Among the muniments preserved in the house in 1910 was a charter of Fulk Paynel, Lord of Bampton (died 1216), granting Bradfield to (Richard) Walrond[1]. The medieval descent of the family is recorded by Sir William Pole (died 1635), whose daughter married Edmond Walrond of the junior branch of the family established at Bovey House, Beer[2]. Richard's son, William Walrond, was a man of standing in the county, whose daughter, Amicia, married Alan Dagville. After Alan's death about 1270 the property at Bovey House passed to Amicia's brother John, son of William Walrond of Bradfield[3]. In 1332 John Walrond, a grandson of William, is found assessed in the lay subsidy at the considerable sum of 5 shillings in Uffculme and 6 shillings in respect of the property in East Devon[4]. In the same year he obtained a licence from John de Grandisson, Bishop of Exeter, to have mass celebrated in his chapel at Bradfield[5] indicating that there was already a substantial dwelling at Bradfield at that date. This is more than a century earlier than the oldest remains in the present house. The fourteenth century building was almost certainly of wood or half-timbered, as were most houses at that date.

Ecclesiastical history

The licence of 1332 leads naturally to a consideration of the ecclesiastical history. In the middle ages, Uffculme was a wealthy church. It had belonged to Glastonbury and had been lost to the Abbey after the Norman Conquest. A charter issued by Stephen in 1136 described the property as the manor of Uffculme, with its churches, chapels, etc[6]. Apart from the parish church there is no indication where these stood but there is no reason to suggest that Bradfield was one of the sites. In 1291 the valuation of the church at Uffculme stood at £17 6s 4d, the highest figure in the Deanery of Tiverton, if we except Tiverton itself, which was divided into four portions each worth rather over £7[7]. The church at Uffculme was therefore a desirable possession.

Rectors of Uffculme were generally non-resident and in the fourteenth century exchanges are recorded with the Precentor and Chancellor, dignitaries in the Cathedral Church of Wells. The Precentor, Richard de Carleton, was instituted in 1336 and granted licence of non-residence for a year for the Rector to attend the obsequies (funeral rites) of the Bishop of Llandaff. Further licences of non-residence, in order to study at Oxford and elsewhere in

England, were granted in 1337, 1338 and 1340. It is not even certain that the Rector was a priest[8]. It can only be concluded that he was an ambitious young man, who regarded his income from Uffculme as a sort of scholarship. The actual cure of souls in the parish would be exercised by humbler priests paid a smaller pittance. Their terms of office varied and they seldom appear in the records. One appears, however, in 1450 when a tax was levied on resident clergy. John Onger was described as parochial chaplain of Uffculme. He would later be called a perpetual curate and had some security of tenure.

At Uffculme, both the Lord of the Manor and the Rector were absentees. This increased the standing and power of the landowners, of whom the principal family was that of Walrond of Bradfield. The licence for divine service to be held in the chapel at Bradfield granted to John Walrond in 1332 was published in common form. A later grant is more fully calendared and more informative. In 1450, Bishop Edmund Lacy granted a licence to John Walrond for divine service (ie the Mass), to be celebrated in his presence in any suitable places in his houses at Bradfield in the Parish of Uffculme, Newland in Cullompton or Bovey in Branscombe. There is the usual reservation of the rights of the parish church concerned[9][10]. The form makes it clear that the grant does not concern a chapel available to the neighbouring parishioners, but a private oratory within the house for the convenience of the grantee and his household. The Mass would be celebrated by a chaplain, who probably also acted as secretary. There seems to be no mention of a public chapel at Bradfield before the time of William Walrond, who was knighted in 1671. In his day, licence was granted 'to publicly read morning and evening prayer in the chapel newly erected by William Walrond, knight, at Bradfield'[11]. This chapel probably stood near the north range of the house. It was replaced in 1874 by the building in the Gothic style which now stands near the public highway. This was also licensed for services in accordance with the rites of the Church of England. The licence was withdrawn after World War II at the request of the owner, the late Lord Waleran, to enable the Chapel to be used without any denominational restrictions.

The house

The house at Bradfield is a complex building of late medieval and Jacobean date, extensively restored and enlarged in mid-Victorian times by John Hayward, architect, of Exeter. After the completion of the work, Hayward read a paper to the Exeter Diocesan Architectural Society in 1862[12]. More recently the writer published a short note with a hatched period plan summarizing a talk given at Bradfield during the visit of the Royal Archaeological Institute in

BRADFIELD HOUSE
UFFCULME

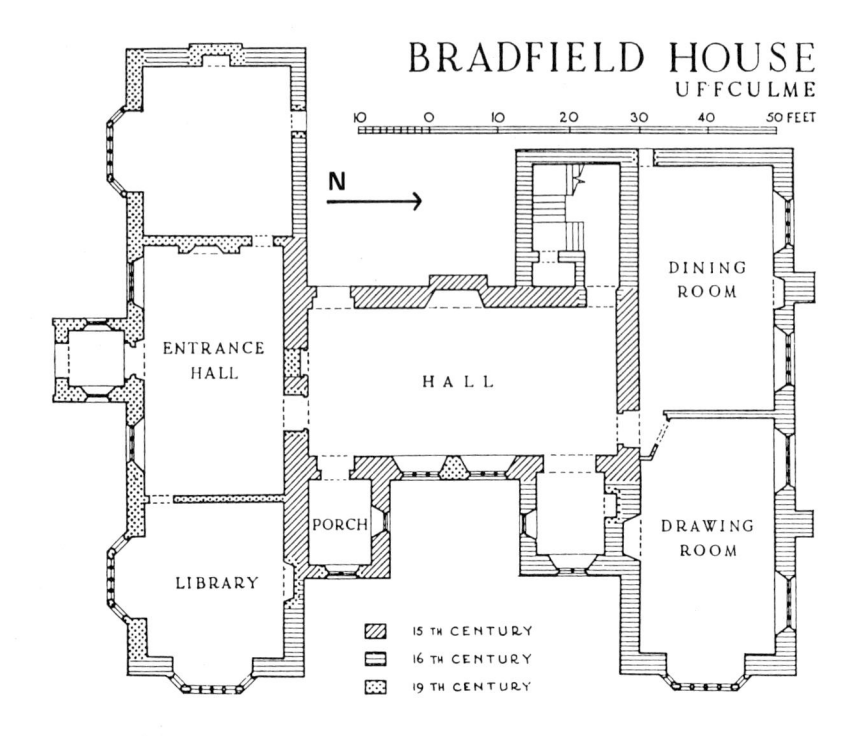

[Floor plan of Bradfield House showing Entrance Hall, Hall, Dining Room, Library, Porch, and Drawing Room, with a legend indicating 15th Century, 16th Century, and 19th Century construction.]

1957[13]. On that occasion, the plasterboard protecting the panelling in the Jacobean rooms was removed, allowing the party to appreciate their full magnificence.

Bradfield is an H-shaped house. The central bar, the oldest surviving part of the building, forms a great hall open to roof level. It dates from the later fifteenth century and was much modified when the Jacobean north range was built in the first quarter of the seventeenth century. Its condition before the Victorian restoration is well illustrated by the drawing, apparently by John Walrond, published by Hayward as one of the illustrations to his paper. The hall must have been accompanied by a domestic range to the north, but the present range and the adjacent staircase retain no features earlier than the seventeenth century. The two ground floor rooms of this date are richly panelled, one with an internal porch, a feature that rarely survives. The south range, containing the medieval buttery and other service rooms, was entirely rebuilt in the nineteenth century to provide additional living rooms with a south aspect. At the same time the main entrance was set in the rebuilt south range, the porch at the southeast corner of the medieval hall being found inconvenient for carriages. The space between the ranges in front of the hall was formed into an Italian garden. There was also extensive planting in the park in which the house was set.

The hall has an elaborate roof of five trusses with richly moulded arches, hammer beams and foliaged pendants. It had badly sunk as a result of the insertion of large Jacobean windows, but was raised to its original horizontal position in the course of the Victorian restoration. The original panelled soffit of the oriel that lit the dais survived, but the oriel itself was later enlarged to form a rectangular recess balancing the porch. The style of the roof indicates a date in the second half of the fifteenth century, but the hall is unlikely to be as early as 1450, when the licence to have mass celebrated was granted to Sir John Walrond. A more likely clue is afforded by the acclamation 'Vivat E Rex' shown in later lettering on the gable above the dais. It probably refers to Edward IV (1461-83). The porch in front of the south-east corner of the hall is contemporary. Normally the room above the porch would form the chapel in which mass was celebrated, but here the room is added with an original window recorded in the wall above the main door.

The existing windows are Victorian, reproducing in part the altered Jacobean openings that existed before the restoration. The only original window surviving at the time of the restoration was a small ogee-headed light, at the west end of the gallery which has now been replaced with a door. The painted decoration shown in the drawing already referred to is also of the early seventeenth century. The royal arms set centrally above the dais includes the Scottish quartering and the unicorn supporter, which were incorporated only with the accession of James I in 1603. The hall now has a high dado of linenfold panelling surmounted by a frieze of Holbeinesque heads, all dating from about 1520-40. Such features would be anomalous in a late medieval hall and its arrangement conforms to the Jacobean alterations. It is possible that this panelling was taken from the dwelling rooms in the north range, contemporary with the hall; but it could well have been brought from elsewhere.

The north range has two rooms on the ground floor with an adjacent stair in a rectangular block tucked in between the range and the west side of the hall. The eastern room, the more richly decorated, has a moulded plaster ceiling and panelled walls with an internal porch providing access from the hall. The plaster ceiling and the woodwork have a close affinity with the Job Room at Bradninch Manor, a few miles away. The work at Bradninch dates from before 1603, as shown by the banner in the trophy of arms on one of the pilasters[14]. There is no such indication of date at Bradfield, but the design is more ornate and the style rather cruder. A date in the first quarter of the seventeenth century would be appropriate. The work was certainly carried out in the time of William Walrond, who succeeded his father in 1586 and was buried at Uffculme in 1627. Contemporary with the north range is the enlargement of the oriel that lights the dais end of the hall. This was extended as a rectangular block to balance the medieval porch and give a symmetrical facade on the east side of the house. The dates 1592 and 1604 on parts of this front probably refer to the completion of structural work, the ornamental panelling being added over succeeding years.

The Walrond family

The direct male line came to an end with William Henry Walrond, who was born in 1762. He married Mary Alford of Sandford who bore two daughters. The elder, Frances, married Benjamin Bowden Dickinson of Tiverton, JP and Deputy Lieutenant, who was High Sheriff of Devon in 1824. It was their son, John, later created a baronet, who was responsible for the Victorian restoration. Hayward's paper was presented in 1862, but Billings, in his Directory of Devon, published in 1857, records the work as already completed. John Walrond was also responsible for the improvement of the park and gardens and the building of the chapel, which still stands. His son, William Hood Walrond, born in 1848 was elected MP for East Devon in 1880. He became chief whip of the Unionist party and Chancellor of the Duchy of Lancaster and was created Lord Waleran. His second and only surviving son, the Hon. Lionel Walrond was elected Unionist MP for Tiverton in 1906. He married Charlotte Coats and they received the Devonshire Association on the occasion of its visit in 1910. He died in 1915 as a result of illness contracted while on service in France[15]. His widow, know to many local people as Lottie Adams, returned to live at Bradfield after 1918.

In 1972, the estate was sold to a development company and the house is now used as a private residential school for maladjusted children. The chapel was subsequently acquired by the Uffculme Trust. Though not owned by the church, the building is used (1988) for a weekly Church of England service provided by the present incumbent for residents in this remote part of the parish.

1. *Trans. Devonshire Assoc.* xlii (1910) 27.
2. W Pole, *Collections towards a Description of the County of Devon* (1791) 140.
3. *Ibid,* 140 and 205-6.
4. The Devonshire Lay Subsidy of 1332, Devon and Cornwall Record Society, new series, 14 (1969), 108 and 44.
5. *Episcopal Registers of the Diocese of Exeter,* ed. F C Hingeston Randolf (cited Ep. Reg.) Grandisson, 652.
6. *The Great Cartulary of Glastonbury,* ed. A Watkin, no 171.

7. Ep. Reg. Bronescombe, 454.
8. Ep. Reg. Grandisson, 809, 838, 908 and 925.
9. *Register of Edmund Lacy, Bishop of Exeter,* Devon and Cornwall Record Society, new series, 13 (1968), III, 59.
10. *Ibid,* 10 (1966), II, 109.
11. *Trans. Devonshire Assoc.* xlii (1910), 30.
12. Exeter Diocesan Architectural Society, Series II, i (1867), 79-84.
13. *Arch. Journ.* cxiv (1957), 143-4.
14. *The Devon Historian,* no 30 (1985), 25-30.
15. *Trans. Devonshire Assoc.* xlviii (1916), 53-4.

Bradfield House from the east, 1985
(Photo G A Payne)

THE VICTORIAN RESTORATIONS OF UFFCULME CHURCH

by Dr Chris Brooks, University of Exeter

IN 1828 the Axminster antiquarian, John Davidson, visited Uffculme church. The town itself had undergone a marked economic decline since the heyday of the cloth industry in the early eighteenth century, but Davidson remarked 'the respectable appearance of the church in what is now so inconsiderable a place'[1]. St Mary's, in 1828, comprised: a nave and chancel separated by a rood screen on top of which 'the mortices remain(ed) in which the figures were fixed which composed the rood and its accompaniments'; north and south aisles, the latter only nine feet wide, but both extending one bay beyond the screen ; a west tower 'forty nine feet high to the top of the battlements', which latter replaced a medieval broach spire that had fallen in the early years of the eighteenth century; north and south porches, and a north east vestry room.

The interior of the church was whitewashed, the clerk's desk and the pulpit with its sounding board stood against the south

The rood screen, with restored central section.
(Photo G H Hall)

arcade, and the nave—filled with high box-pews—was galleried on three sides. The galleries in the south aisle and at the west end of the nave dated from 1631 during Humphrey Steare's incumbency, that at the west end of the north aisle was erected in 1721 when John Windsor was vicar. Effectively then, the nave formed an auditorium, spatially discrete from the chancel and having the pulpit as the visual focus for the congregation. Davidson would have found the overall disposition of the nave entirely familiar, for such an arrangement could have been found in countless English parish churches at that time. It was the product of the need to modify and adapt an inherited medieval building—its plan the product of pre-Reformation Catholic worship—to the requirements of post-Reformation, and particularly eighteenth-century, Anglicanism. Rather than the liturgical focus being the eucharist and the altar, the Hanoverian Sunday service was centred on the sermon and the pulpit. By the early years of the nineteenth century communion was generally celebrated only four times a year. So, in 1828, the Uffculme nave and aisles formed an auditorium for sermons and the long chancel beyond the screen was functionally all but redundant.

The Oxford Movement and the Camden Society

The major changes that took place at Uffculme in the twenty years following Davidson's visit stemmed directly from national changes both in the character of Anglicanism and in the nature of ecclesiastical architecture. The 1830s saw the Oxford Movement bring about a resurgence of High Church principles within the Church of England. The Tractarians, as the Movement's adherents became known, stressed the Catholicity of Anglicanism, the importance of the sacraments, and the sacramental office of the priesthood. Simultaneously, the revival of Gothic architecture—which had been underway since the second half of the eighteenth century—entered a new phase, largely influenced by the writings of Augustus Welby Northmore Pugin. Pugin insisted that Gothic was the only legitimate style for church building and that the Gothic adopted should be both historically accurate and expressive of the doctrine and liturgy of the Church Catholic. Tractarianism and Puginianism came together in 1839 with the founding of the Cambridge Camden Society, later known as the Ecclesiological Society. The theological doctrines advocated at Oxford impled liturgical innovations that, in their turn, would involve a complete change in the nature of Anglican church design.

The Camdenians set themselves no less a task than that of bringing about this change: contemporary church interiors had become mere 'preaching-boxes'; the clutter of galleries and box-pews that filled them should be swept away. Churches should again embody and symbolise Catholic principles, with the emphasis not upon preaching but upon the sacraments: consequently, the physical focus of the interior should be shifted from the pulpit to the altar. New churches should be designed in a historically accurate Gothic. Medieval churches—suffering from several centuries of decay, makeshift repairs, and inappropriate alterations—should be restored. These developments are reflected with striking fidelity in the changes made to Uffculme church in the late 1830s and 1840s.

Early changes

The first of these changes, in 1839, was unremarkable enough. A new gallery was erected entirely filling the north aisle, with further sittings for school children erected on top of the screen. The work was undertaken for simply utilitarian reasons: the increase in Uffculme's population over the first decades of the century, made additional accommodation necessary. Almost all trace of this work has now disappeared, but two aspects of it are important: the financing and the architect responsible. As well as pews financed, and therefore owned, by individual parishioners, the gallery contained a number of free seats. The funding for these came almost entirely from four people: £40 was given by Richard John Marker; £20 by the vicar, the Reverend George Townsend Smith; £10 each by Dr John New and his son John New Jnr[2]. Marker (died 1855, aged eighty seven) lived at Yondercott House. He owned land in the parish, though not on a large scale and his wealth seems to have derived from his profession as an attorney and, perhaps, his marriage to Anna Windsor (died 1834, aged eighty one). Anna was the sister of Smith's predecessor as incumbent, the Rev'd James Windsor, and thus both the daughter and grand-daughter of earlier vicars of Uffculme. As well as this close family connection with the church, Marker was also one of two owners who leased the rectorial glebe from the Prebendary of Uffculme, whose stall was at Salisbury[3]. In consequence, as we shall see, Marker seems to have assumed certain responsibilities for the physical upkeep of the Uffculme chancel. The Rev'd G T Smith had been instituted into Uffculme in 1833 and as he rebuilt the vicarage at a personal cost of over £2000[4], he was evidently a man of some means. The News were from Bristol, where John New snr had practiced as a doctor. Like Marker, then, to whom he was close in age, he was a professional man. In the parish the family owned both Craddock House and Yondercott, where they were Marker's immediate neighbours, although, like his, their holdings in land were not particularly extensive[5]. What we seem to have in Marker, John New snr and Smith is a professional élite—the Law, Medicine, the Church. Their association was to be fundamental to future work on the church.

The north aisle gallery was erected and fitted out by William and John Veals, who received £125 14s. 8d. between them for the contract. The Veals or Vealls family were Uffculme carpenters, members of the family also periodically filling the office of parish clerk. The use of immediately local sources of skill and labour for church-building work, often on quite a substantial scale, was regular practice up to the early decades of the nineteenth century. But increasingly effective communications, the growth of the architectural profession, and the ever more sophisticated ecclesiological ideas of the 1830s broke up this traditional pattern of employment. Expertise was sought from farther afield and, as the building accounts show, everybody else who was employed on the work of 1839 came from outside Uffculme. Samuel Knight, an experienced ecclesiastical mason from Exeter, was employed to move wall monuments from the north aisle; Robert Beer, an Exeter decorative artist and glass painter, painted the Royal Arms that still survive at the west end of the church. Most important of all, however, was the appearance of Mr Hayward, Architect of Exeter, paid £6. 6s. 0d. for his 'plan of the Gallery'. This was John Hayward (1808-1891), who was then at the beginning of his long career and who was to become the leading ecclesiastical architect in the south west. He played a significant role in the mid-Victorian restoration of Bradfield. A Londoner by birth, Hayward took up residence in Exeter in 1835 and, by 1838, was practicing from 50 High Street, Exeter as an architect and surveyor. The gallery at Uffculme is one of his earliest documented works. Such details are suggestive of changing attitudes. Nevertheless, the scheme of 1839 was essentially conservative, maintaining—and indeed extending— the 'preaching-box' character of the interior. Things were not to remain so for long.

Major changes, 1843

The next stage in the Victorian development of the church took place in 1843 and was quite different in character. Documentary details are incomplete, but an entry in the vicar's commonplace book gives the essentials:

> 'In the year 1843. The Chancel was rebuilt with improvements by the Lessees of the Rectory and on that occasion the new Font of Caen Stone carved by Knight was placed in the Church at the equal cost of the Vicar and Mr New amounting to £50.—The Statuary work of the Chancel was also done by Knight.'

Richard Marker, as we have already seen, was one of the lessees and it may be assumed that he was the moving force in the rebuilding. The work was structurally comprehensive. The chancel walls were rebuilt, a new roof was provided, and an impressive east window erected. The motives behind this programme of work are evident from the character of the improvements mentioned in the account quoted above. All are concerned with enrichment, with re-establishing the chancel as the visual and architectural climax of the interior. As such, they are responsive to the High Church desire to reinstate the eucharist—and therefore the sanctuary—as the liturgical core of Anglicanism. The chancel roof was given a keeled barrel vault made of plaster, originally stencilled and powdered with stars, with an enriched bay over the altar to give the character of a ceilure. A new Gothic reredos was erected, taking the entire width of the sanctuary east wall below the sill and rising to either side of the window. The visual concentration upon the sanctuary established by the ceilure and reredos is reinforced by the pattern glass filling the east window, the brilliance of its colour—like the original stencilling of the chancel vault—deliberately contrasting with the whitewash, stained wood and plain glazing of the rest of the interior at that time. The focus for this east end ensemble is, of course, the stone altar, relatively small, but intricately ornamented with appropriate symbolic devices. In the centre an Agnus Dei (figure of a lamb, emblematic of Christ, bearing the banner of the cross) flanked by finely detailed trails of vine and corn, with sacred

The stone altar.
(Photo C Stokes)

monograms filling the outer bays. Both in style and conception, the intricately-detailed font stands as a companion-piece to the altar. Like the reredos and altar it was carved by Samuel Knight, who had been employed at the church during the work of 1839.

The character of the work of 1843 interestingly exemplifies a transitional stage in the development of Victorian ecclesiastical design. Although stylistically committed to Gothic and executed with considerable skill, the work does not follow those prescriptions of Pugin and the Camdenians that demanded fidelity to historical examples and modes of construction. The overall forms of Knight's reredos, altar and font do not have historical precedent; their details are highly selective—the reredos even incorporating classical scrolls with Greek inscriptions. The chancel vault is not, of course, a vault at all, for, being made of plaster, it performs no structural function. On the other hand, the theological complexion of these renovations is clearly to be identified with High Church principles. The rebuilt chancel, with all its fittings and decoration, provided new a focus for worship and an elaborate setting for eucharistic celebration. The ornate new font gave physical expression to the parallel importance of the sacrament of baptism.

Legality of the new altar

The association of Marker, Smith and New in funding—and presumably initiating—the work identifies them as forming a High Anglican party in the parish. The changes they effected at Uffculme are recognisably Camdenian: the shift of focus to the chancel, the adoption of symbols and emblems in the decoration of the new work, the general emphasis upon what came to be known as 'Sacramentality', were all key elements in the programme of the ecclesiologists. This is confirmed by what is clearly the most 'advanced' of the Uffculme improvements—the stone altar. Fixed altars were a particular object of protestant detestation, and the attempt to reintroduce them into Anglican churches was one of the most controversial items in the Camdenian programme. When, in 1843, the Society tried to install a stone altar in St Sepulchre's, Cambridge, the result was a notorious law case which ended with the Dean of Arches declaring the altar to be in contravention of the canons of the Church of England. In such a context the Uffculme altar, also erected in 1843, was daring and, had it been challenged, its legality must have been dubious. Already, however, there were precedents for such fittings in Devon. Most important of these were the church of St Andrew in Exwick, consecrated in 1842, and its mother church of St Thomas: both had elaborately embellished sanctuaries in which a stone altar was the centrepiece. The architect of Exwick and, probably, the designer of the St Thomas sanctuary, was John Hayward. The vicar of St Thomas, and the moving force behind both schemes, was the Reverend John Medley. Medley was closely associated with the Camdenians and, in 1841, had founded a local sister society to the Cambridge Camden, the Exeter Diocesan Architectural Society. In the following year Hayward became its honorary architect. The Society advocated the full range of ecclesiological principles and the success of Hayward's career, particularly in the 1840s, is closely related to its growing influence. Given the nature of the changes made at Uffculme in 1843, it is not surprising that both Hayward and the Society played central roles in the final stage of the early Victorian work on the church. Nobody from Uffculme appears in the Society's List of Members for 1842 or 1843. No list for 1844 exists, but by 1845 both R J Marker and G T Smith were among the membership, and in that year the Society's Committee visited St Mary's.

Report of the Visiting Committee

The Committee found a church in which a 'preaching-box' nave existed side by side with the new liturgical provision of the recently rebuilt chancel. Their report[6] is clearly directed towards encouraging further restoration, but restoration in which ecclesiological views on Gothic style and structure should be more fully implemented. Accordingly, they praised the 'the very liberal spirit' behind the chancel restoration, but found some 'matters of detail' injudicious. In particular they regretted the 'mere imitation' represented by the plaster vault. Nevertheless, encouragement rather than rebuke was needed: after all, Marker and Smith, who had been largely responsible for the restoration, had recently become members of the Society, and a lot remained to be done at Uffculme. The nave was still 'much cumbered with heavy galleries' and the tower, shorn of its spire, was 'in a very dilapidated state'. Neatly enough, the final words of the Committee's report praises the 'spirit of restoration . . . which has animated some in the parish', and suggests that an appropriate expression of that spirit would be the rebuilding of the tower and spire. Action was not long in coming. By the time the report was printed in 1847 a footnote could be added in which the Committee remarked, 'with the greatest pleasure', that 'very extensive restorations and an enlargement' were underway and that 'all the work is to be well done'. The Committee had good cause for pleasure and for some confidence, for, as we shall see, the funding of the new work at Uffculme was in the hands of the small High Church group already identified—two of whom were, of course, members of the Society—and the architect of the restoration was to be the Society's own John Hayward. On 2 January 1846 'Plans and Specifications from Mr Hayward for the enlargement of the Church'[7] were laid before a parish meeting and accepted. A

Restoration Committee was set up with Smith as chairman and including New and Marker, who was to become vicar's warden during the course of the restoration. Work on the church started later in the same year.

1846-48 restoration

The 1846-48 restoration at Uffculme falls into two major parts: the enlargement of the church by the addition of an outer south aisle, and the rebuilding of the tower and spire. Hayward's aisle is of five bays, the same length as the far narrower medieval south aisle, from which it is divided by an arcade on the line of the original south wall. The style Hayward adopted is early Perpendicular with big three-light windows set back from the wall plane under heavy hood moulds. In a skilfully handled design, the vertical accents established by tall windows and buttresses are balanced against the broad porch in the second bay and the horizontal emphases of plinth moulding, string course and long, unbroken roof-line. Internally, Hayward modelled his arcade on the Perpendicular arcade to the medieval south aisle, covering the new aisle with a fine waggon roof, historically accurate and left unceiled in a conscious display of structural integrity. In the south aisle itself he retained the original medieval flat roof, perhaps renewing some timbers, certainly introducing a number of Norman corbel heads— apparently found in the masonry of the old south wall. The new outer aisle provided sufficient accommodation to allow the south aisle gallery to be removed, after which the whole of this side of the church was reseated with open benches.

When the medieval tower was taken down the west walls of the aisles collapsed and Hayward took the opportunity to design the west end exterior as an integrated whole presenting a show front to the town. The steeple, designed in a mature Decorated style with an angle-buttressed tower and a stone broach spire, impressively tops the steep hill that drops down to the Culm and forms the focus of the west front ensemble. Internally, alterations converted the west gallery to an organ loft, and the singers who would have used the gallery were provided for by choir stalls in the chancel. In addition, Hayward designed a new vestry and a new boundary wall for the churchyard, including an impressively craggy lich-gate to the south west.

Both because of its extent and the quality of its craftsmanship, the 1846-48 restoration involved spending a lot of money. The final financial statement shows a total outlay of some £3524[s]. Of this a mere token of £85 was raised by means of a church rate levied on Uffculme parish as a whole and £15 was subsequently added in part-payment for the new vestry. Odd subscriptions, including £50 from the Walrond family, raised little more than £200. All the rest of the expenditure on the restoration, amounting to nine-tenths of the total cost, was met by the High Anglican triumvirate of Smith, New and Marker. Dr New contributed £225 to the building of the outer south aisle, with a further £65 coming from other members of his family. George Smith paid £50 towards choir seating and new flooring in the chancel, contributed £250 towards the aisle and bore the cost of the new boundary wall and lich gate, an additional £214. Richard Marker paid for the whole rebuilding of the west end of the church, including the tower and spire, recasting the bells, and the new clock—a total of £1700. Along with Smith, he paid £50 for the chancel improvements; finally, he cleared the deficit of £640 on the building of the outer south aisle.

What they got for their money was much more than a smartly renewed parish church. Hayward's studious use of historically correct Gothic, with its high finish and careful expression of structural integrity, was a conscious expression of principle. If, as Pugin and the Camdenians insisted, Gothic was the architectural language of the Church Catholic, then here at Uffculme the very style was a deliberate statement of Catholic values. Internally, the process started by the chancel rebuilding and improvements of 1843 was furthered decisively. Removing the south gallery and altering the west put an effective end to the old 'preaching-box' disposition of the nave. The open benches erected in the south aisles established a precedent for doing away with the box-pews so detested by all good ecclesiologists. In 1850 all the remaining pews were replaced by open benches on the same pattern as those introduced in 1846-7[9], arranged so that the whole congregation faced towards the sanctuary and the altar. The pulpit was moved to the north, and the font repositioned in a baptistry area by the south door, where it was held to symbolise the doctrine that the sole entrance to the Church was through the sacrament of baptism. With these alterations, the process of change was itself complete, and Uffculme's architectural and liturgical identity fixed until the present century.

1. John Davidson, *Church Notes,* 5 vols., MS (1828-1849), West Country Studies Library, Exeter, s726, 5 DEV/DAV. The Uffculme entry is in the *East Devon* volume, pp. 557-563; subsequent references are to this account.
2. Among the Uffculme parish records in the Devon Record Office is a commonplace book containing notes on the church and parish, DRO 1920A/P116. It was started by the Reverend James Windsor in 1810 and contains important details of Victorian work on the church; details of the financing of the gallery are taken from this source.

3. In 1839 Marker owned 234 acres, largely agricultural land, which he rented out; he also leased 63 acres of the rectorial glebe: DRO *Uffculme Tithe Map and Apportionment*.
4. William White, *History, Gazetteer and Directory of Devonshire* (Sheffield, 1850), p. 329.
5. In 1839 Dr John New owned 225 acres, 177 of them being occupied and presumably farmed by his son, John New jnr who owned a further 93 acres in his own right, most of which he seems to have farmed himself. Both men are entered in the Tithe Apportionment as 'landowner of property': DRO *Uffculme Tithe Map and Apportionment*.
6. 'Report of Visiting Committee, read at a quarterly meeting of the Exeter Diocesan Architectural Society, holden in the College Hall, Exeter, November 13, 1845', *Transactions of the Exeter Diocesan Architectural Society*, vol. 2 (1847), pp. 119-32: the quotations that follow are all from this source.
7. Minutes of parish meeting, 2 January 1846: *Vestry Minutes 1839-78*, DRO 1920A/PV2.
8. DRO 1920/P116 contains an itemized summary of expenditure on the work of 1846-48, with a subscription list; the account is signed by Smith as vicar, by Marker as one of the churchwardens, and by William Wood as the other. All details of financing come from this source.
9. A faculty petition for reseating was entered 5 June 1850: DRO 1920A/PW46.

One of the Norman corbel heads that support the roof of the inner south aisle.
(Photo G H Hall)

UFFCULME BAPTIST CHURCH
by Christine Snell

THE Baptist Church is long established in Devon. A congregation existed in Moretonhampstead in the sixteenth century and in 1649 Abraham Cheare, a pastor in Plymouth, was gaoled in Exeter for three months for his 'non-conformity' and for encouraging religious assemblies.

The Act of Uniformity of 1559 caused wide dispersal of non-conformists to rural areas but not until after the Act of Toleration of 1689 do we hear of Baptist congregations in the Culm Valley. In 1700 the 'old hall' at Prescott, close to the Quaker Meeting House at Spiceland, was licensed for worship and a society was established in Cullompton as a branch of the Baptist Church of Upottery. Until 1745, Upottery, Prescott and Cullompton shared one pastor. A chapel was built at Saint Hill, near Blackborough in 1816, the society being formed mainly from members from Cullompton.

Little is known of the Uffculme church's early history as most of the records have been lost but it, too, once had close connections with the Prescott church and later with Saint Hill. The first church was probably built at the beginning of the 19th century. The present building consists of random stone walls, rendered on the east and part south elevations, slate roof with vents and simple arch-headed stained glass windows.

Grave headstones on the north and south sides date from the early 1800s. They include those of:
Samuel and Mary Baker (d 10 June 1829 and 18 March 1832)
John Buffett Tucker, 'Minister of the Gospel' (d 12 Nov 1888)

and several members of the Sparkes family:
James and Elizabeth Sparkes of Wellington
Samuel and Edith Sparkes
Samuel and Elizabeth Sparkes of Coldharbour (d 18 April 1905 and 15 April 1876)

The date on the present gate is 1815, but the entrance was once higher up the hill to provide direct access to the main door. The change was made some time in the nineteenth century. Cottages owned by the church that were once on the opposite side of the road were demolished and the land transferred to Poynings on condition that a wall was built. This was done, but in recent times it has been taken down.

The church can seat approximately 150 people including the gallery seating. The gallery once accommodated the choir and organ. Staircases on each side of the entrance porch led to the gallery but one staircase was removed some years ago because of wood beetle. Doors at each side of the pulpit lead to a small meeting room that was formerly the vestry. Above this, a room of similar size, once used for the Sunday School, is now a general purpose room. During World War II, soldiers were billeted in it. Boards on the main church wall above the pulpit can be removed, if required, to further enlarge the church.

The Tiverton & District Free Church Council Gospel Mission Van in the Square, about 1910.

UFFCULME UNITED REFORMED CHURCH

ACCORDING to tradition, in the latter half of the seventeenth century local non-conformists (or Dissenters) used to meet for worship in secret on Gaddon Down. Eventually a building was erected for public worship on a site near Fox Brothers woollen mill at Coldharbour. It is not clear whether or not this was on the site of the present United Reformed Church, but in 1720 the Clarke family of Bridwell House seem to have been responsible for the erection of a chapel on this site. When a reconstruction took place in 1862, a foundation stone was discovered bearing the date 1720 and the names RICHARD and MARY CLARKE. This stone was recut and built into the north wall. It is now enclosed above the ceiling installed in the 1979 rebuilding.

The chapel was 'independent' for many years, and did not become affiliated to the Congregational Church until 1923. In 1972 the local congregation accepted integration with the Presbyterian Church of England and became part of the United Reformed Church.

Reverting to the early history of the chapel, the first minister is recorded as being the Reverend Samuel Short in 1705. He was followed by John Chorley, who built and resided in Bengal House in 'Church Street'. At one stage the Clarke family introduced a Reverend John Williams, a Unitarian, as minister, but his teaching was not appreciated by the congregation. The story goes that when he rose to speak the choir would commence singing. The Clarkes, therefore, took Williams into their house and built a chapel in the grounds. A list of ministers from 1705 to the present day does not contain the name of John Williams.

The original building was of cob, the interior unplastered, with tin sockets to hold candles. In the early nineteenth century farmers came on horse-back with their wives riding pillion and stabling was provided at the east end of the chapel. This part was incorporated in the main building about 1830, to provide a schoolroom. Children were charged ½d (one half-penny = 1/5p) per week, but the then minister stopped this practice.

A separate school building was constructed in 1891 on the opposite side of Commercial Road, there being at that time ninety children attending with seven teachers. During World War II, the school was occupied by the military and returned to church use in 1946.

Bengal House had remained the manse until 1924, when it was sold and a new manse built next to the church on land purchased for a nominal one pound from Mr Clarke of Bridwell.

As the school building had not been used as such since the mid-1970s and the manse was no longer required, due to a grouping of local United Reformed Churches, both buildings were sold to provide funds for the interior reconstruction of the church in 1979. The old school building is now a private residence.

From notes compiled by the late Miss Margaret Batting, an Elder of Uffculme United Reformed Church.

TRADE AND INDUSTRY IN UFFCULME 1850-1939:
As seen from the Local Directories
by Adrian Reed

TOPOGRAPHICAL descriptions of counties, often with route maps, became popular from the early eighteen hundreds. These normally included some historical accounts of the towns and larger villages and of the principal economic activities in and around them. The seats of the nobility and gentry were listed and the names of mayors and MPs noted; but no one else's. By the middle of the century, however, the great improvement in communications brought about by the penny post and the railways opened up to commerce and to the private traveller almost every part of the Kingdom. Classified directories were published to cater for their needs. White's, Billings', Kelly's, Harrod's and the Post Office's own directory all followed a similar format—a description of the town or village followed by lists of residents. In the earlier editions the lists were divided into 'Gentry' and 'Traders' and in the later ones between 'Private Residents' and 'Commerical'. The names of big local landowners, men and women of independent means, retired officers of the services and Church of England incumbents appeared as private residents. Doctors and lawyers were regarded as 'Commercial', together with everyone working on his own account or acting as manager or agent for someone else. The directories, therefore, give a very good indication of the range of economic activities in a village but it is necessary to look to other sources for the numbers of employees in trade, industry and on the land.

Uffculme, described rather unkindly in the older volumes as a 'decayed market town' and in the later ones as being 'pleasantly seated on the river Culm' had reached its population peak with 2,098 inhabitants at the census of 1851. By the end of the century the total had slowly declined to 1,704 and was to remain at about that figure until the nineteen seventies when it again began to grow, to reach 2,027 at the 1981 census. Throughout that period it maintained the same mix of agriculture, service industries and manufacturing that, with variations in proportion, it has today.

Agriculture

Agriculture, primarily pastural, has always been the main component of the economy of this very large parish of over six thousand acres. The numbers of those noted as farmers remained at about thirty five for the whole of the second half of the nineteenth century but for some reason increased after nineteen hundred so that between 1910 and 1939 there were usually forty four or forty five people described as such. Dependent largely on agricultural work were the blacksmiths and wheelwrights. They were fairly evenly spread throughout the parish. Uffculme in 1857 had two of each and Ashill one wheelwright and two blacksmiths. Stenhill and Hayne had their blacksmiths and Craddock a wheelwright. Bradfield, which was largely the Walrond estate, would have had its own craftsmen while the other small hamlets were within easy distance of their larger neighbours. Saddle and harness makers were concentrated in the village where there were three. One veterinary surgeon resided in the parish and Ashill had the services of a 'horse and cattle doctor' who was also a shopkeeper. Fifty years later in the early nineteen hundreds there were five wheelwrights but the number of blacksmiths had dropped to two. More surprisingly, the saddlers and harnessmakers had disappeared except for an enterprising lady who had added saddlery to her bookselling, ironmongery and stationery business. As the horse was still the main means of transport power, either the cobblers were mending tack or the business had fallen into the hands of bigger men in Cullompton or Tiverton. A few years later a saddler again appeared in the lists, but that the parish could support only *one* saddler is surprising.

Shopkeepers

In the nineteenth century, England was still very much Napoleon's 'nation of shopkeepers' and Uffculme was no exception. In 1857, there were twelve of them as well as five shoemakers and five tailors some of whom may have sold items they themselves did not make. In addition, there were three butchers and three bakers, while several of the seven dairymen were not farmers selling their own products direct to the customer. These businesses were not limited to the main village. Ashill, for example, had three shops and the small hamlets of Stenhill and Hayne one each. Geographically, the distribution meant that everyone was within walking distance of a shop. In 1857, the only two main settlements without one were Craddock and Bradfield. Both these were the demesnes of wealthy families and their households were within easy reach of Uffculme and Kentisbeare respectively.

Until World War II there was no great change in the number of shops. There were three butchers in 1857 and three in 1939 and the same number of bakers. Specialisation, however, began to creep in. Drapers, grocers and ironmongers appear but it is well into the twentieth century before a greengrocer is noted. By 1910 there was a fishmonger and a Co-op. The general store, though, predominated throughout the period.

Other trades

There was considerable economic fluidity. Shops opened and closed at will and some unlikely occupations were combined with shopkeeping. In 1873 Craddock had its post office and shop run by a pig dealer while twenty years later a local veterinary surgeon was also a beer retailer. Perhaps the latter business grew from successful use of the product with horses!

There were many more self-employed craftsmen in the middle of the nineteenth century that at its end. Some trades obviously died out. There would not be enough work for the patten maker when leather became cheaper. The number of masons and carpenters dropped by half. This may have been due to the improvement in housing and the arrival of the building contractor who would be able to offer the range of skills required in the construction of the newer type of house. One craft that shrank was that of cooper, presumably because of the lessening demand from farmers for storage casks for salted meats and because of the bottling of beer.

By the end of the nineteenth century, Uffculme was becoming much more sophisticated. Railway travel from the late seventies put visits to the shops and theatres of Exeter within the reach of all but the poorest. By 1890 there were three ladies' dressmakers in the village and more than one hairdresser. As well as the newsagent and the bookselling ironmonger there was even a stall of Messrs Whyman's at the railway station. There was a chemist's shop, no doubt offering what would now be called 'toiletries'. By 1906, a bicycle dealer was in business to be followed not long after by the first garage. More sedentary diversion was provided by the inns of the parish. Early in the period one dropped out, but four others still welcome their guests today.

Manufacturing industry

Manufacturing industry in Uffculme was based initially on waterpower while, later, coal supplies were assured by the railway. In the 1850s the parish had two large worsted/woollen spinning mills, at Coldharbour and at Bradfield. The former owned by Messrs Fox of Wellington, closed as late as 1981 and is now preserved as a working Museum. Bradfield Mills did not survive the eighteen-sixties and all traces of the large buildings have now disappeared. There were two other mills, both operated by waterpower, the Town Mills which burnt down after World War II and Hackpen Mill, near Ashill, which went out of business half a century before. Both were flour mills.

Until the end of World War I, the Uffculme Steam Brewery, owned by the Furze family, was an important employer of local labour. New buildings were erected in 1857 at the east end of the village and for the next seventy five years the Brewery's tall chimney dominated Uffculme, as did that of Fox's Mill the hamlet of Coldharbour to the west. After 1918, the heirs of the Furze family gradually shed their interests. They disposed of the dozen or so public houses which they owned, stopped brewing and turned to mineral water production before they finally sold out altogether. Although the chimney and the brewery machinery have long since gone, the buildings remain as a prominent feature of the Uffculme skyline. Over the past half-century or so they have sheltered a bewildering number of commercial enterprises ranging from cidermaking to a dolls' hospital. A chronicle of their fortunes would provide an interesting commentary on the ups-and-downs of small industries in rural England.

The three main employers of labour in Uffculme—the Town Mills, Coldharbour Mill and the Brewery left a firm imprint on the shape and character of the village. The Bradfield Mills lasted too short a time and in any case must have looked mainly to Kentisbeare and Cullompton for their labour while Hackpen Mill was too small to have had any marked effect. Apart from the buildings themselves, all three principal mills provided some housing for their employees. The terrace of cottages in Mill Street was dependent on the Town Mills at the end of that road while the Brewery had rows of rather more substantial houses at the top of East Street. But these were small scale in comparison with the results of Fox's undertaking at Coldharbour. Here they erected some substantially-built dwellings which formed the nucleus of a large hamlet with its own inn and shops. When town gas came into general use the supply from the mill's own plant lit Coldharbour while the village proper got its supply from the privately-owned gasworks established near the river bridge in 1871.

Communications

Although in the period being considered roads and bridges had been much improved, communications have always been of great importance to Uffculme, lying as it does some distance from the bigger markets. The coming of the railway was especially important to local farmers. Droving of stock by seller or buyer ended. Live cattle could be sent where prices were good and dairy products marketed fresh. By the time the railway closed, the lorry and the tanker had long since taken over the farmer's business from the train. For the farmer's wife, the rural bus service which developed between the wars must have been a most welcome breach in her isolation just as the programme of rural electrification removed a great deal of the drudgery from her life. Today the bus service is following the railway to extinction and the motor car is becoming the only guarantee of mobility. The cycle agent of 1906 would find few customers eighty years on!

Looking back over the ninety years of this brief review the main impression is one of a division between the manufacturing and service industries and agriculture which changes proportionately very little over the period. By the end of it there were fewer self-employed craftsmen but there were more firms to employ them directly. Shops have become more specialised and begun to concentrate in the main village and to leave the hamlets, but they are larger and now have paid assistants. Manufacturing industry continues to be made up of one big employer giving work to 130 or more people and a number of smaller ones. Agriculture does not change greatly although there are more farmers at the end of the period than at the beginning. In fact, there has been very little change in the economic structure of the parish. Where most change has occurred is in the social fabric—but that is another story.

COLDHARBOUR MILL

by Linda Cracknell

COLDHARBOUR Mill is one of a few surviving reminders of Devon's industrial connection with wool. The West Country industry became enormously important nationally during the seventeenth and early eighteenth centuries, but subsequently experienced a decline and has been relatively unimportant since. It is this which makes Coldharbour Mill particularly interesting. Although not established until 1797, it continued production well into the twentieth century.

The West Country industry

Devon's woollen industry was based on its famous kersey and serge. Kersey was a cheap plain-coloured, coarse-textured cloth made

Memorial to James Hollway, clothier, died in 1632 and his wife Joan, died 1645.
(Photo G H Hall)

from local wool, mainly for the home market. Two of the principal manufacturing areas were the Culm and Exe valleys and evidence of this can be seen in the churches of Cullompton and Tiverton, which were extended and decorated by local kersey clothiers.

The West Country was probably better known, however, for the manufacture of serge—a light cloth made with a worsted warp (for strength) and a woollen weft. The changeover from kersey to serge manufacture was brought about by changes in fashion and by the rise in production of worsted yarn. This was made possible in the sixteenth century by the longer fleeces grown by the sheep due to enclosures and by the introduction of the more sophisticated 'Saxony' spinning wheel.

Tiverton was one of the main manufacturing towns, but wool markets were known in Cullompton and Bradninch as well as Uffculme.

Coldharbour Mill and Fox Brothers
From the late seventeenth century the Were family made serge in the Wellington area. Like other clothiers working in the domestic system, they bought raw fleeces which they delivered to their cottage workers, using company waggons and journeymen, collecting the spun yarn or woven cloth. The waggons also transported finished yarn and cloth to Topsham for shipment to London and Europe.

In 1745, Edward Fox, a Cornish Quaker, married Anna Were, also a Quaker. Their eldest son Thomas joined his maternal grandfather in Wellington and was soon made a partner. When, later, his brother Edward joined him, the name of the company was changed to Fox Brothers. In 1782 Thomas married Sarah Smith, the daughter of a Quaker banker from London. The Fox Brothers developed two factories at Wellington and, in 1797, Thomas Fox bought and started developing Coldharbour Mill.

The Domesday Book records two mills at Uffculme. The precise location of these is uncertain, but it is *possible* that one was on the present site of Coldharbour Mill. It is thought that there was a paper mill here—the earliest known reference is to a Tom Norton, paperman of Coldharbour, in 1707. In 1753 a great flood damaged the mill and it was rebuilt sometime afterwards.

Trewman's *Exeter Flying Post* for December 4th, 1788 advertised:

'To Let, Grist Mills at Coldharbour Mills, Uffculme, lately built entirely new, with a very large head of water'.

It was this mill that Thomas Fox bought as a site for his woollen manufacture because it was ideally situated by the River Culm and had a reliable source of water. He wrote to his brother Edward:

'I have purchased the premises at Uffculme for eleven hundred guineas, which I do not think dear as they include fifteen acres of fine meadow land. The buildings are but middling but the stream is good.'

In 1799 Thomas Fox started to expand Coldharbour Mill, a bold move at a time when the great woollen industry of the West was in decline. He wrote of his plans to his builder:

'I have some intention of erecting a building at Coldharbour to serve at present merely for spinning, but which might at any future time be converted . . . I wish therefore to make my building three stories high . . . and to place the wheel nearly at one end so as at any time to add to it another building of like dimensions.'

Products

Fox Brothers were able to expand because they responded to a growing demand for 'long ells', lengths of fine, white serge, heavily fulled, measuring twenty five yards long by an ell (thirty one inches) wide and weighing twenty one pounds, which were exported to the colonies and China through the East India Company. In the late eighteenth century 'long ells' became the main output of the Wellington mill, replacing the continental trade which had been greatly reduced. However, the 'long ells' trade was hit by the crippling export duties imposed to pay for the wars with the French.

Design on the canvas wrappers used in the despatch of cloth from Fox Brothers. It was in the style of a Royal Arms to help ensure safe passage.

Seeking additional home markets, Thomas Fox developed a flannel, a soft woollen cloth which he exported to the Americas. In keeping with his Quaker pacifism however, he refused to sell the material to the East India Company when he learned that it was to be used for gun cartridges. However, Fox Brothers accepted a profitable military contract later in the century.

In 1881, a Parliamentary Commission decided that the British Army uniform should be changed after the terrible losses sustained in the Zulu and Boer Wars when the famous scarlet tunics made the troops easy targets. After much deliberation, a new colour was selected for camouflage—khaki. Fox Brothers obtained a commission for the manufacture of 5,000 pairs of puttees in this new colour. The Quakers justified the contract because not only would it create employment but the new colour would, they hoped, save lives. Spinning worsted yarn for puttees became the main activity at Coldharbour Mill until it closed.

Motive power sources

Water power satisfied all the factory's needs until the second half of the nineteenth century though Thomas Fox certainly investigated the possibility of steam power and was visited by James Watt in 1782. However, he was always concerned to maintain full employment in order to relieve increasing poverty in the early nineteenth century. He wrote of this to a colleague in Darlington:

'I make it a point to spin all worsted I use by hand to employ as many of the poor as possible.'

When the factory changed to worsted production and new combing machinery was installed in 1865 extra power was needed. It was then decided to use steam power at Coldharbour Mill. Two twenty five horse power beam engines were installed to supplement the water power—one in 1865 and a second in 1890. They were replaced in 1910 by a powerful Pollit & Wigzell three hundred horse power horizontal, cross-compound steam engine, which, together with the water wheel (which was used for night shift working until 1978) supplied all the factory's needs until its closure.

Employees conditions

From the late eighteenth century, bread prices increased sharply, and during the late 1780s Thomas Fox conducted a survey of living conditions in Wellington. This showed that about six shillings of a weekly income that seldom exceeded ten shillings was needed to buy bread. In an effort to ease this burden he opened a shop for his workforce in Wellington selling food, fuel and basic clothing, on a non-profit-making basis. Rice was also imported through the East India Company as a substitute for bread.

Houses were built near the mills for the workers to rent cheaply; this helped ensure a constant workforce, and generally improved living conditions. Many of the cottages in Coldharbour were built for this purpose. Workers were summoned at the start of the day by the mill bell which rang five minutes before work was due to start.

Fox Brothers never employed children under the age of eight years. This was initially a self-imposed restriction as Parliamentary Acts regulating the employment of children in the industry were not passed until into the nineteenth century. Education Acts of the 1870s made it compulsory for children to be educated until ten years of age, but some children continued to work as 'half-timers'. This meant that they worked at the Mill for two or three days of the week and attended school for the remainder. Between 1891 and 1895 the Factory Register records seventy children from Uffculme aged between ten and thirteen years working at Coldharbour Mill. All had to be passed fit to work by a doctor who checked that they were not incapacitated and were at least ten years of age.

Fox Brothers opened a Mens' Institute in Uffculme for their male employees at Coldharbour. Unlike similar institutes, drinking was not allowed on the premises and it was mainly for recreation and games.

Final decline

The effects of the recession in the woollen industry resulted in Fox Brothers being forced to close several of their departments in the early 1980s. One of these was their worsted spinning unit at Coldharbour which was closed in April 1981. At the time there were forty people working full-time in the Mill. Soon after this, the Coldharbour Mill Trust was formed to save the buildings and to preserve some of the textile machinery and power sources. The Mill is now open to the public as a Working Wool Museum.

A fuller account of the history of the mill, with references and suggestions for further reading, is available from the Coldharbour Mill Museum, Uffculme, Devon EX15 3EE.

UFFCULME WORDS AND DIALECT
by Jack Gollop

MY formative years were spent in Uffculme in the 1920s and it was not until I went to school at Tiverton that I discovered that the language spoken by the average person in the village was not universal. Later, when working in London, I realised that Devonians pronounced and used many words in a somewhat eccentric fashion compared with other parts of the country. For example, they might say 'drekkly' for 'directly' and *mean* 'latter on' rather than 'immediately'. I also discovered that the Devonian accent varied from place to place. When I visited the Ponchydown Inn at Blackborough just after the War two things astonished me. Every other customer had a dead rabbit or a game bird dangling from his person and the conversation was, at least at first, quite incomprehensible to me. A sample is contained in Ronald Webber's *Devon and Somerset Blackdowns*—'Cass'n see z'well's cou'st, cas't?' (You can't see as well as you used to, can you?).

The advent of wireless must have done a lot to familiarise country folk with 'Oxford English'. The following story illustrates how easy it was for 'bilingual' Devonians to lapse into the vernacular. A farmer's daughter who was undergoing nursing training (and learning to speak 'proper') returned home for a holiday. When greeting her mother she said 'Is that the cat that was a kitten when I was home last?'. Her mother replied 'Ees me dear' and the daughter then said 'Caw, an 'er grawed'.

Another story, no doubt intended to illustrate the superiority Devonians feel in relation to lesser beings who have one language only concerned a well-spoken motorist from 'foreign parts' who stopped while travelling in Devon to ask the way. He was amazed to be given directions in a posh voice. On enquiring where the yokel had acquired his accent he was told 'Well, ectually I cut my mouth on a broken bottle'.

My interest in local speech was re-awakened when I read the examples reproduced in the booklet *Culmstock: A Devon Village* and I have since looked at other lists. It is interesting how much pronunciation varies, eg Devon, Debben, Deb'n, Dem and also how much spelling varies as writers struggle accurately to reflect accents. Meanings vary, too—'Skat' can mean 'to throw away' or 'a passing shower'. Meanings sometimes change over the years. 'Smeech' originally meant 'a smell', particularly from a fire. Later it came to mean 'dust' or 'smoke'. Sometimes words in fairly general use seem to acquire special meanings locally, witness the use of the word 'clever' to mean 'good'. Some colloquialisms are not peculiar to one locality. Thus 'napper' is shown in some lists as a West Country word, but it also crops up in the Cockney song 'Any Old Iron?'.

Many of the words and phrases in the Culmstock booklet were common in Uffculme. The following is a list of additional words and sayings in use in Uffculme some fifty years ago. It does not pretend to be comprehensive and other people will have their own favourites. Some words and sayings may also be considered 'local' in other parts of the country.

Addle aided—slow witted
Agone—past, as in yers agone = a long time ago
Aps—abcess
Apse, to—to close, as in apse the door or gate
Arten—aren't you

Barney—argument, row
Bread and scrape—bread and thinly spread butter, previously bread and point
Blackhead—boil

Cack handed—awkward
Call home, to—remember, particularly to remember a person, eg 'can't call 'e 'ome'
Can't odds it—can't change it or do anything about it
Car—carry
Chap or boy-chap—young man or sweetheart
Covey—man, character. Frequently, artful covey
Clever—in good health. More often 'none too clever' to indicate indifferent health
Crack-on—pretend, give false impression or to move on quickly
Cruel—very, eg ' 'urtin' summat cruel'

Daishels—thistles
Dap—bounce, hop or go quickly
Demps—dusk
Dissen—don't you
Doughbake—somewhat dim person
Dough fig—dried fig
Drangway—pedestrian way
Drekkly—later on
Dripnybit—threepenny piece
Dug—dog
Dummon—woman

'eaving—sweating, as flagstones on a change of weather
Ees or Aiss—yes

Faggot—disparaging term for cantankerous person
Fair to middling—not too bad

Fair to poor—not too good

Gake—stare in somewhat bewildered fashion
Gakey—somewhat stupid
Gert—large
Gyte—trick or habit generally peculiar to one person
Guzegobs or guzegogs—gooseberries

Hoozen—windpipe
Hummick—large slice or piece

Idden—is not
Iteming about—fooling around
Item—trick

Jonnick or jonic—pleasant, agreeable, straightforward

Kutchee—modified version of the earlier kutchee pawed = left handed
Kirtcher—mysterious part of the anatomy liable to be strained when lifting

Larruping—untidy, thin, tall
Leather, to—beat, chastise
Let in to—strike heavily
Lew—shelter
Lights—lungs. One time, human lungs; later, more likely animal lungs after slaughter
Long dog—greyhound
Loopy—slightly eccentric

Masterpiece—something good or out of the ordinary; not in art but in nature
Measly—unsatisfactory or mean
Mommet—obstinate, obtuse or awkward person
Mumpheaded—stupid
Mummelheaded—foolish

Nattlings—chitterlings
Nothing—not nearly, eg 'nothing like good enough'

Opeway—opening or entry large enough for carts
Ow be scatting vor?—How are you getting on?
Ow ert thee?—How are you?

Peart—very cold (weather)
Peersif—it seems as if
Presently—later on
Proper—large, excellent
Puggled—confused, slightly deranged or something done to be awkward

Raked up—dug up from the past

Rames—remains, eg of poultry
Right away—immediately
Ropey—not up to standard. Originally applied to cider when thick and sour
Rough scat—rough cast
Rubbige—rubbish

Sawny—a bit odd
Scad, scat, scud—passing shower
Scammeling—awkward, unco-ordinated
Scrimp, to—economise, usually 'scrimp and save'
Skat—to fling
Skammel—to walk badly
Skeeming—cutting daishels (thistles)
Skimmished—drunk
Slapdash—liquid coating for a building
Slewed—drunk. Usually used in 'half slewed'
Smeech—originally a smell, particularly from a fire. Later dust or smoke with particles in it
Snitch—nose
Spider blinding—whitewashing a ceiling. Probably local derivation of the earlier 'bug blinding'
Strake, to—stroll, mooch
Straakin'—wandering without purpose
Strawmawt—length of straw for drinking through, especially from a cask

Tiddivate—bedeck, prink out
Tidden—it is not
Tiddly—mildly drunk
Tizzy, in a—upset, worked up
Twad'n—it wasn't

Ugsed—hogshead
Upsidaisy—get up, stand up

Valled—fell
Vices—fists

Werse bin?—where have you been?
Wert about?—what are you doing?
Werebeto?—where are you?
Wissen?—won't you?

Yerawl—ear

Zackly—exactly
Zamzawed—overcooked

Some publications on Devon dialect:
> *Devon Verbal Provincialisms*—A T Gregory
> *The Devonshire Dialect*—Clement Marten (Revised Edition 1974)
> *Peasant Speech of Devon*—Hewett
> *A Dictionary of Devon Dialect*—John Downes
> *A Dialogue in the Devonshire Dialect*—J F Palmer (The first book in the Devon dialect, 1837)

INNS, TAVERNS AND BREWING IN THE PARISH OF UFFCULME
by Jack Gollop

A GREAT deal of information can be obtained about inns and taverns in the parish of Uffculme from various directories that were published from 1850 onwards. Before this, very little seems to have been recorded. For example, no trace has been found, to date, of the Fountain Tavern which is known to have existed or The Stump which, according to some people, was situated near the lower corner of The Square. A map of 1765 shows The Stag and Hounds at Stag Corner, Bradfield, but it is not known when this ceased to be an inn.

In the 1850s there were eight public houses in the parish. These included the following four which still exist as such:

The Commercial Inn, subsequently the Commercial Hotel and now the Ostler.

The George, at one time the George and Commercial.

The Lamb Inn, and

The New Inn, Ashill, now the Ashill Inn.

There were also the London Inn (delicenced in 1986), the Half Moon in High Street, exactly where is not known, the Star Inn in Coldharbour and the Farmer's Hotel, now a private house at the bottom of Clay Lane. The Half Moon and the Star Inn appear to have closed about 1880 and the Farmer's Hotel during World War One.

Landlords' other occupations

Several of the inns had other businesses associated with them. In 1850, there was a smithy at the Commercial Inn. In 1856, the inn doubled as the Inland Revenue Office and in the late 1870s and 1880s, the landlords of the Commercial Inn were also butchers. The butchers' shop is believed to have been in what is now the public bar that overlooks the Square. One of the landlords, Mark Luxton, moved the butchery business from The Commercial to Fore Street in what is now the fish and chip shop. In 1893, the next landlord of the Commercial was a builder.

In the late 1870s the landlord of the Lamb Inn was a farmer. Both the Farmers' Hotel in Uffculme and the New Inn at Ashill were run for many years by innkeepers who were also veterinary surgeons. In 1850, the landlord of the London Inn was also a shoemaker and for many years in this century the inn was also a dairy.

The Farmer's Hotel on the corner of Clay Lane, before its conversion. Parts of the building date from about 1500.

Some families have had very long associations with some of the inns, notably the Jones family with the Farmers' Hotel from the 1850s until World War I after which the surviving member of the family, Sydney, carried on a harness maker's business at the rear of the hotel. He also kept pigs and was popular with children as he bought acorns from them for his pigs at twopence per peck.

The Welland family was associated with the London Inn from the 1880s until the 1950s.

Furze & Co

With regard to the actual ownership of the inns there is little on record beyond details in the census returns from 1841 onwards, some details of which are given on page 37 in the contribution by P Regardsoe. V G Barnard, in a pamphlet *Inns of the Tiverton Area* states that Furze & Co were probably founded in 1850 at the London Inn, Uffculme. It is understood that William Furze came to Uffculme from Wellington and first started a mineral water factory in Clay Lane in what is now Heather Mews Cottage. The artesian well sunk nearby is said to be as deep as the church spire is high. William Furze built the Steam Brewery in 1858.

When William Furze died in 1891 his executors continued the business until 1903 by which time a number of inns in the area were in their control. The business was auctioned in 1903 and bought by

Starkey, Knight and Ford. Starkey, based at North Petherton, Knight based at Bridgwater and Ford from Tiverton having amalgamated in 1895.

As far as premises in the parish of Uffculme were concerned Starkey, Knight and Ford owned the London Inn, the Commercial Hotel, the Lamb Inn and the New Inn, Ashill. The George was owned by the Heavitree Brewery, Exeter. Starkey, Knight and Ford were taken over by Whitbread in 1962.

Much (congenial) research is needed on the actual buildings used as public houses. An Inn is shown at Lamb on very old maps. However, the present building is quite modern and it is believed that the original was destroyed by fire.

An outing from the George Hotel in the early 1900s. The Fiat 14-seater char-à-banc was owned by A S Western of the Uffculme Garage.

GRANTLANDS
by Pamela Gibbs

GRANTLANDS, a grade II listed building, is a large Victorian house and associated outbuildings, now divided into a number of individual dwellings. It was built in 1864-65. The architect is unrecorded but was probably John Hayward.

The main building, with walls of random rubble limestone and Beer stone dressings and complex tiled roofs, was offered for sale by auction at the Half Moon Hotel, Exeter, on the 4th June 1890 by Messrs Knowlman and Wood. The sale notice in *The Times* of 10th May described the property at that date:

> 'Devonshire, Uffculme—The very beautiful Freehold Residential Estate, known as Grantlands, situated in the parish and adjoining the village of Uffculme, five minutes walk from the station, two miles from Tiverton Junction, 16 from Exeter, and 4½ hours from London. It embraces an area of nearly 33 acres and comprises a very superior stone-built residence, of pleasing elevation, approached by a winding carriage drive, with lodge at entrance, and containing spacious entrance halls, four well proportioned reception rooms, 17 bed and dressing rooms and complete domestic offices: capital stabling for 12 horses, together with a model farmery, with comfortable residence built in character with the mansion, beautiful pleasure grounds, charmingly laid out and well matured, with conservatory, two greenhouses, and large range of vineries and peach houses, also three good kitchen gardens. The park and meadow lands are well timbered and slope gently to the River Culme, which affords boating and trout fishing.'

The group of buildings can be seen clearly from the footpath that follows the course of the former Culm Valley Light Railway. From the south, the mellow grey stone buildings appear much as they must have done a century ago.

Origins

The name 'Grantland' appears in the Devon Protestation Return for Uffculme Parish in 1641, when a John Grantland was recorded, and his name appears again in a 'lease for life of church house' in 1651. In 1661 he was granted a transfer of lease of land relating to Ricks Park, Park Meadow and The Hamms in the Parish of Uffculme, and his name is seen again in the Parish Register of 1669.

It is firmly believed locally that there was originally a farmhouse on the present site of Grantlands, to which the house was added in 1864, this date being carved on one of the exterior walls. However, no trace has been found in the records of any farmhouse on the site and the stone used and architectural features of all the buildings seem to be much the same.

The description of the property published in 1890 mentions a 'model farmery' and further sale particulars in 1919 refer to a 'farmery' which included a shippen for four cows, a piggery and fowl houses, a hay barn and a granary, and this may well be the basis of the belief that there was originally a farmhouse on the site. In fact they formed part of the whole complex when built and the word 'model' is perhaps significant.

Owners

The 1866 edition of Kelly's Directory lists the Reverend G T Marker (vicar of Uffculme) as the occupier of 'Grantlands Mansion' and it therefore seems very likely that it was he who built the house in 1864. The 1871 census return shows that he and his wife were still in occupation, together with a number of servants. Mrs. Alice Marker's scrapbook is deposited in the Devon County Record Office but it contains no reference to the house or its occupants. Subsequent occupiers of the house were a Mr H Paget and then Arthur Ayshford and Juliana Wood, whose son Henry's death at sea is recorded in a memorial in the parish church.

In 1890, the mansion with its seventeen bedrooms, two dressing rooms, and 'a magnificent ash staircase' was purchased by the Rev'd Stephen Bennett. In 1919, the property was again on the market and was sold at auction to Mr Henry Hugo Worthington. He died in 1924 but his widow Amelia remained in occupation with a number of servants, including a butler and a chauffeur for her Rolls-Royce. When she died in April 1939, the contents of Grantlands were sold. These included three paintings by J W M Turner.

The Grounds

These were originally laid out by Messrs Veitch and Son, whose founder, John Veitch, had, a century earlier, laid out the park at Killerton for Sir Thomas Acland.

Estate agents' particulars of the sale in 1919 are particularly interesting and include details of the extensive gardens with tennis and croquet lawns, two summer houses, camelia and peach houses and two vineries. The grounds extended down to the river, and there was a private walk to the station. A stream running through them was crossed by a 'picturesque bridge', and there was a small boathouse at the junction of the stream with the river. The agents' particulars refer also to 'that portion (of land) known as Ham Meadow', which is interesting in relation to the reference to 'The Hamms' back in 1661.

Water was supplied by wells and there was a windmill (pump) in the garden, probably near the site of the present Markers development. A long-time resident of Uffculme, the late Jack Denner, recalled that his father, Sam, remembered this windmill as he was a gardener at Grantlands during World War I. The head gardener always wore a hat and a green baize apron as his badges of office. The lawns were so extensive that a pony was used to pull the mower.

Gardeners at Grantlands, about 1905. The second gardener from the left is Sam Denner.

Wartime changes

On the outbreak of war in September 1939 the house was used first as a convalescent home for British troops and later, from November 1943 until May 1944, as headquarters of the US 17th Field Artillery Observation Battalion who nicknamed it 'The Castle'. Officers and some NCOs were based in the house, 'other ranks' being quartered in nissen huts and tents in the grounds. From Uffculme, the Battalion left to take part in the D-Day landings.

At the end of the war, the property was taken over by developers, who among other things, removed the 'magnificent ash staircase' and converted the front portion into two flats and the rear into houses. The surrounding buildings were also converted for residential use though their former uses are in some degree still apparent, particularly in the house called 'The Granary' where an outside stone staircase can still be seen leading to the first floor where the grain was stored. Part of this house was clearly originally the dairy. Other buildings were the garage for three cars, the coach house, the agent's house, a small building which was the butchery, and the Lodge at the main entrance.

The whole estate must have been, and indeed still is, an area of quiet charm, though nowadays the camelia houses, the boat house and the head gardener in his hat and green baize apron have all vanished. John Veitch and his sons would doubtless approve though, of recently-planted specimens of Erica x veitchii—a tree heath hybrid discovered in their nursery about 1905—which thrive in the sheltered, slightly acid soil of Grantlands.

Grantlands from the south-east, c1905.

THE US 17th FIELD ARTILLERY, OBSERVATION BATTALION AT GRANTLANDS
by Gordon Payne

COMMANDED by Lieutenant Colonel J G Harding, the battalion (part of V Corps) arrived at Gourock on the Clyde in the ss 'Fairisle' on 4th November 1943. It then travelled by train to Uffculme where it was billeted at Grantlands, nicknamed 'The Castle'. The house was used as headquarters, officers' and NCO's quarters and mess. The remainder of the battalion was quartered in a combination nissen hut and tent camp.

For the European landings, the main bodies of all units left Uffculme on 16th May 1944. Headquarters battery and 'B' battery travelled to Falmouth, 'A' battery to South Wales and service units to the Bournemouth area. From D-day plus two to VE Day the battalion drove from Omaha Beach in Normandy to Sisice in Czechoslovakia.

'The History of the 17th Field Artillery, Observation Battalion' published by Lowman & Hanford Co of Seattle contains much detail of their movements and actions and a full list (roster) of personnel. Photographs of various activities are provided, mostly in Grantlands, which, at that time, had several Redwood conifers and a summer house. Baseball was played on the tennis lawn and parades appear to have been held in the fields between the house and the mill leat.

Also shown are PC Knowles on a bicycle, a waggon of Wigan coal at Uffculme station, the Brewery (with oast house and bridge over the road), the George Hotel, the London Inn and not least a bomb crater at Bradfield House!

The book contains posed photographs, with everyone identified, of all units and groups—mostly taken on the south side of the house. A copy is in the possession of John F Maney of Van Wert, Ohio who, with his son Kevin, revisited Grantlands in June 1984.

THE CULM VALLEY LIGHT RAILWAY
by Jack Gollop

AN account of the Culm Valley Light Railway is given in the booklet *Culmstock: A Devon Village* published by the Culmstock Local History Group in 1982. The notes below concern the line and its traffic within the parish of Uffculme.

The project was launched at a meeting held at the George Inn, Uffculme on 15th May, 1872. The committee appointed to promote the undertaking included five prominent Uffculme men and one of these, William Furze, who owned the brewery, became one of the seven directors.

Construction

Construction began in 1874 and the line was completed in 1876. The railway played a vital role in the life of the Culm Valley from 29th May 1876, when passenger services were inaugurated, until 1963 when passenger services were withdrawn. The line continued to be used for milk tanker trains to and from the milk factory at Hemyock until 1975. Part of the track bed is now used to provide a pleasant footpath between Coldharbour Mill and Bridge Street.

The line was constructed on a 'light' scale. The surface of the terrain was followed nearly all the way, thus minimising the need for expensive bridges, embankments, cuttings and other works. As some landowners were reluctant to sell land for the railway, the hedges of fields were followed wherever possible. These constraints meant that there were some unusually tight bends on the track as well as weight and speed restrictions.

Initially, the engines and the carriages were specially built or adapted for the line. The engines were either 2-4-0 (no 1298 and no 1300) or 0-6-0 (no 1376 and 1377) side-tank engines and the first carriages were four-wheeled. Later carriages came from other GWR lines. The train was known in Uffculme as the 'Puffing Billy'. Another nickname was the 'Hemyock Express'. In the Culm Valley, GWR meant 'Go When Ready' and the expression 'Linger and Die' was also used to describe the line.

Traffic

The 1920s were probably the busiest years for the station at Uffculme. In the morning and evening, the two passenger carriages were nearly always full. Many adults travelled to work at Exeter, Taunton and Tiverton and places in-between. Schoolchildren from Clayhidon, Hemyock, Culmstock and Uffculme used the train to attend Tiverton Middle School. In the summer, a special train was hired to take Sunday School outings to Exmouth or Teignmouth. This necessitated extra carriages and on one occasion this proved too much for the engine on the one-in-sixty six incline out of Tiverton Junction. The train was reversed into the siding at the Junction to take a longer run and eventually succeeded in getting up the incline to the accompaniment of delighted cheers from the children, many of whom were hanging out of the windows despite the stream of smuts from the locomotive.

During these years there was heavy traffic in coal, mainly from South Wales. This included coal for the gas works in the Leat, for the steam brewery and for most of the houses in the district. It was the practice of many of the larger houses to buy coal by the truck-load (ten tons). Distribution from the station was by horse and cart. Another important freight was grain for the corn mill, then a water mill at the east end of the Leat. A large slaughterhouse to the west of the station (on the site now occupied by the feed mill) also generated a good deal of traffic. Special trains brought hundreds of animals, mainly sheep and lambs, from livestock markets all over the West of England to be slaughtered for Smithfield. The carcases were conveyed to London by rail from a siding specially constructed alongside the slaughterhouse.

The Station, Uffculme. G. Crease, Photographer.

On a somewhat smaller scale there was a lively trade in rabbits. Several men earned a living by trapping, netting or shooting them and they were collected, packed in wicker crates, and despatched by rail to London. Not all the rabbits left Uffculme, however. Rabbit was quite a popular food locally, especially among poorer families, hence the jingle 'Does your mother want a rabbit, skin and all for ninepence?'. At this time considerable quantities of eggs were sent by rail from Uffculme, mostly from a collecting depot at Ashill.

Pigeons also featured in the freight handled by the line. However, these were the racing variety which travelled in wicker baskets. Some were despatched from Uffculme for distant stations where they were released at pre-arranged times to race home. One famous bird 'arrived' in Uffculme only to discover that the race had been cancelled because of bad weather. Other consignments of pigeons arrived by rail at Uffculme Station to be released there by the staff.

At this time milk was usually transported in churns and most farms were expected to convey it to collecting points. The milk factory at Sampford Peverell provided such a collecting point in the Leat adjoining Uffculme Station. This was a large shed built on stilts so that loading and unloading could take place at a convenient height.

All kinds of general merchandise were brought by rail to the village together with building materials, paint, distemper and plumbing materials. These were collected by the consignees or delivered by an employee of a local merchant in a light spring waggon. Another important service was the bulk supply of newspapers. Morning and evening papers arrived at Uffculme Station for the village. By this time Coldharbour had its own halt (opened in 1929) for passengers and a siding mainly for the supply of coal to the mill.

Operation

Uffculme always had its own 'railway children', usually groups of small boys who were fascinated by the line and its equipment. Particular interest was created in the early 1920s when two divers worked in the river to the east of the station to replace an old pile bridge with an iron one. Normal activities by children included applying an ear to the rail in an attempt to ascertain from the vibration how far away the train was and placing a penny on the rail to see how it expanded under the weight of the engine. Some favoured lads were allowed to practice morse code on the signalling equipment which connected one station with another. The small huts built beside the railway for the gangers who maintained the track were a constant attraction. To discourage too close an interest some train crews had a jolly habit of scattering hot cinders or directing a jet of hot water from the 'pet' pipe on the engine as they passed.

Generally, the line appeared to operate in what might be described as an air of unhurried efficiency to which no doubt, the

MAY 1876

First, Second and "Parliamentary" Classes

Tiverton Junct.	6.50	9.35	12.40	4.30	6.45
Uffculme	7.09	9.54	12.59	4.49	7.04
Culmstock	7.24	10.09	1.14	5.04	7.19
Hemyock	7.35	10.20	1.24	5.15	7.30
Hemyock	8.30	10.35	3.00	5.25	7.45
Culmstock	8.46	10.51	3.16	5.41	8.01
Uffculme	9.01	11.06	3.31	5.56	8.16
Tiverton Junct.	9.15	11.20	3.45	6.10	8.30

JULY 1929

First and Third Classes

Tiverton Junct.	8.45	11E40	11S40	12.50	4.40	7.00	9S00
Coldharbour Ht.	8.54	11E49	11S49	12.59	4.49	7.09	9S09
Uffculme	8.57	11E52	11S53	1.02	4.52	7.12	9S13
Culmstock	9.21		12S02	1.17	5.05	7.26	9S23
Hemyock	9.45			1.38	5.16	7.37	9S33
Hemyock	7.42	10.25			2.45	5.40	8S10
Culmstock	7.53	10.35		12S07	2.55	5.50	8S21
Uffculme	8.03	10.50	12E10	12S17	3.10	6.05	8S31
Coldharbour Ht.	8.06	11.00	12E13	12S20	3.19	6.08	8S34
Tiverton Junct.	8.15	11.12	12E28	12S29	3.31	6.19	8S43

SUMMER 1963

Second Class only

			★			★	
Tiverton Junct.	8E45	9S20	11S25	11E25	1.42	5.10	
Coldharbour Ht.	8E55	9S30	11S35	11E35	1.52	5.20	
Uffculme	8E58	9S33	11S39	11E39	1.55	5.23	
Culmstock Ht.	9E22	9S55	12S00		2.06	5.34	
Whitehall Ht.	9E38	10S10			2.15	5.43	
Hemyock	9E43	10S16			2.20	5.48	
		★	★		★		
Hemyock	7S10	7E15	10.30			2.45	6.00
Whitehall Ht.	7S15	7E20	10.35			2.50	6.05
Culmstock Ht.	7S22	7E27	10.43		12S09	2.59	6.13
Uffculme	7S33	7E38	10.54	12E20	12S20	3.11	6.24
Coldharbour Ht.	7S36	7E41	10.57	12E25	12S25	3.16	6.28
Tiverton Junct.	7S47	7E52	11.10	12E38	12S38	3.27	6.39

E: Except Saturdays; S: Saturdays only; ★Passenger only.

Some typical timetables of the CVLR.
(from 'The Culm Valley Light Railway' published by Branch Line Handbooks, 1964)

speed limit of fifteen to sixteen miles per hour contributed. The trains almost invariably ran to time and connections at Tiverton Junction were met, but as the number of daily journeys was limited to four or five in each direction the pressure was not very heavy. One engine driver, Dollfuss Hawkins, found time to stop the train between Uffculme and Culmstock to catch rabbits in purse nets which he made himself. Crews would also stop the train by Yondercott Farm to take on board potatoes and eggs which they had purchased. One of the schedules allowed a lengthy time at Uffculme for shunting and at least one crew found that this afforded them an opportunity to visit the London Inn. If they looked like being late for their scheduled departure the Station Master gave them a friendly toot on the engine whistle whereupon they ran down Bridge Street to resume their duties.

In the line's heyday, the Station Masters were gentlemen who made a considerable impression. Messrs Lake, Teague and Cockram immediately spring to mind. In addition to Dollfuss Hawkins, engine drivers who gave long service on the Culm Valley included Percy Rouse and Anthony Richards. One of the best remembered porters was Bill Chilcott, probably because he could both yodel and play cricket, although not at the same time.

Sadly, after World War II, road transport increasingly took over the traffic enjoyed by the railway and the justification for its existence gradually disappeared. It was a very sad day when it finally closed. Not only had it played a vital part in communications and the provision of employment, but the view of the train as it steamed along and the noises of the engine—its whistle and the screech of tortured metal as it negotiated the bends—contributed significantly to the character of the Culm Valley.

The following articles on the Culm Valley Light Railway provide technical detail for those interested.

B K Cooper, *Railway Magazine,* vol 78 (1936) pp. 116-120, 423-426
P W Gentry, *Railway World,* vol 14 (1953) pp. 38-40, 119
R C Riley, *Railway World,* vol 23 (1962) pp. 369-372
B K Cooper, *Railway World,* vol 37 (1976) pp. 106-108, 357

A useful account is provided in a booklet *The Culm Valley Light Railway* by R Crombleholme, D Stuckey and C F D Whetmath, published in 1964 by Branch Line Handbooks.

CRICKET IN UFFCULME
by Jack Gollop

WITH the exception of one minute book, the records of the Uffculme Cricket Club have been lost or destroyed and it is not possible to say with certainty where or when cricket was first played in the village. However, according to some notes made by the late John Adams of Coldharbour, the game is believed to have been introduced to Uffculme in 1852 by a gentleman called Woodward. Adams wrote 'The play, of a rustic description, took place in the Manor Grounds of a Mr W T Wood, Gaddon, and was between young gentlemen from Ayshford Grammar School and employees of the neighbouring Blackborough Scythe Stone Quarries, then a thriving industry'. This tends to bear out a newspaper report in 1926 which quoted Mr H G New, who had played for the Club, and who was President from 1926 until 1939, as saying that there had been a continuous history of cricket in Uffculme for sixty years before World War I.

Bridwell and Yondercott have been mentioned as possible locations for cricket grounds and it is known that the game was played in the field adjoining Chapel Hill opposite the new entrance to Poynings. In the late 1890s Mr Samuel Sparkes secured the old Wellington Cricket Club pavilion for this field, a new one having been erected in Wellington in memory of Mr Harry Fox who had lost his life climbing in the Caucasus. In 1905, the Uffculme Cricket Club raised over one hundred pounds to move this pavilion and provide a new pitch in the field which is now the main sports field of the 'Top School' and which was then owned by the Williams family. Cricket was also played in a small field behind Ayshford when it was the Grammar School.

Early matches

We do not know a great deal about early matches. However, the September 1879 Parish Magazine contains a record of three of them, two against Killerton Park and one against Wellington. All were lost. Uffculme's most consistent player was the Rev'd Arthur Hillyard, a curate, who opened the batting and bowled lobs. Most of his victims were clean bowled. John Adams' notes state that the Rev'd Hillyard, who became rector of Upton Pyne near Exeter, may rightly be said to have put the game of cricket in Uffculme in the ascendant. During his time the Club possessed a number of 'skilled and painstaking players and proved for many years a match for any rivals'. Mr Adams records that the year 1895 was a phenomenal one in which the Club won all its matches.

Whilst the actual results of village cricket matches played in the last century are of limited interest, the names of some of the players and the teams played are worthy of note and the sports reporting is entertaining. In 1897, for example, the Uffculme team included two Wellands (F and J), two Tanners (W and the Rev'd T), and two Furzes' from the family that owned the brewery. Opponents were mainly from Tiverton, Cullompton and Wellington. Press comments included 'Uffculme fielding slack', 'the Uffculmites gave a splendid exhibition' and (to explain a defeat 48-78) 'Sampford had two foreigners and Uffculme were weak with absence of Spencer (Capt) and others'. During this season, H P Larkins, formerly Uffculme's captain, scored 122 not out for them against Blundell's 'B'. Uffculme sent a Second XI to Bradfield and lost heavily. Possibly they were overawed by the status of opposition, which included Lord Southwell, Lionel Walrond and Dr Tracey.

The years immediately before World War I would have been of great interest but the only match reports available are those sent in by opposing teams at Tiverton. Two Wellands (F and J) were playing at this time, plus H G New and, at least once, a gentleman called Quatah Uddin Khan, a name not terribly common in Devon.

Post-war decline

The War caused a gap of some twelve years in Uffculme's cricket. John Adams records, sadly, that 'many a gallant player were among the slain. The accoutrements of the game were sold up as there was no-one to be found to carry on'. Eventually the Club reformed in 1926 at the instigation of the Rev'd J F Prowse, curate, and C N (Charlie) Levett and returned to the field owned by the Williams family for a rent of four guineas per season, including use of the pavilion. One of the Secretary's first tasks was to arrange for the scything of the pitch. As an act of faith, no doubt inspired by the curate, fund raising was left in abeyance pending replies from the Vice-Presidents. Only members were permitted to practice.

From this time until 1939 fixtures and results steadily improved. The teams played were mainly local but included sides from Exeter and Taunton. Uffculme fielded two Wellands and three, occasionally *four,* Trevelyans.

The 1939 season appears to have been marred by bad weather if not by the approaching hostilities. The brief notes which exist of two committee meetings held at the close of the season, after the outbreak of war, refer to uncertainty about the future of the Club but do not mention the actual reason! In 1940 it was decided to carry on and to allow soldiers billeted in the village to join the Club for a fee of one shilling. However, the minutes of a General Meeting held after the war record that the Club had been forced to cancel all its fixtures in 1940.

New grounds

When World War II ended there was no long delay as after the First World War. In April, 1946, a meeting produced sufficient support to justify re-starting a Club. There was a major snag as the Williams family had to impose restrictions on the use of their ground. As a result it was decided to move to a field, then owned by the Disney family, which adjoins what is now the Coldharbour Mill car park. Because of ditches this was not ideal and after a year or so the Cricket Club moved to a three-acre field adjoining Gibraltar bungalow which is now part of a much larger field.

The late 1940s and early 1950s saw a steady improvement in the facilities at 'Gib'. A pavilion was built and extended and the ground and wicket rapidly improved. Most of the work was done by the members themselves and, although on the small side, 'Gib' became a delightful cricket ground which rapidly gained a good reputation. The subsequent improvement in the fixture list was made possible by the excellent wickets (and teas) that the Club was able to offer and was helped also by the appointment of F C Doidge, headmaster of the Primary School, who had been Secretary of the Club, as Secretary of the Devon Club Cricket Association.

The Club colours were changed in 1948. Before the war they had been green and yellow. The new caps were white with a blue and gold badge embroidered with the letters 'UCC' and a 'duck'! This was an oblique reference to earlier rivalry between Culmstock (the 'baas') and Uffculme (the 'ducks') when taunts about sheep stealing had been the order of the day. Ironically the badge was designed by a Culmstock artist, Peter Earland, and unkind critics said that the duck looked more like a goose, and one in an interesting condition at that. This may have had something to do with the earlier rivalry or, more likely, the paucity of the artist's fee—seven and sixpence!

Revival in performances

During the 1950s and early 1960s Uffculme had an unusually strong side for a village. Most of the opposing sides came from towns rather than villages and there were regular visits from touring teams including Bangor, Chelsea, Sandu (Birmingham), Southall, Southampton, Staffordshire Pirates, Sun Life of Canada, Thetford Wanderers and Wiltshire Moonrakers. As wickets improved so did individual performances and centuries were scored quite often. With the exception of the Trevelyans, the families that had been prominent in the earlier history of the Club were no longer represented. However, for much of the time there were two Disneys, two Doidges, two Gollops and two Tolleys (uncle and nephew).

An Uffculme XI which played on the County Ground, Exeter in a match for the 1950 Benefit of groundsman, Cyril Rawle.
(L. to R.) Frank Chick (Umpire), Dick Palfrey, Bert Disney, Arthur Hellier, Sam Disney, Peter Doidge, Clifford Harding.
Russ Trevelyan, Peter Williams, Graham Gollop, Jack Gollop, Paul Doidge.

The 1963 season saw some remarkable individual performances, particularly by D Lindsay and R Owen, but it was only an average season as far as results went. Sadly it turned out to be the last season for eighteen years. On 29th April, 1964, the *Devon and Somerset News* reported that 'Due to lack of players, Uffculme CC has decided to close down for the season'. This was only part of the story. It had, in fact, become impossible for the dwindling band of enthusiasts to sustain the standards achieved earlier. Eventually the Club was wound up. The assets were frozen for five years, in case there was a move to re-start, and then disposed of to help other sporting activities. This was a sad end to an organisation which had given great pleasure to many people: players, helpers and supporters. Even more regrettable was the fact that soon there was little to show for the efforts of countless enthusiasts who had contributed to Uffculme cricket over a period of a hundred years. Hard work on at least three different grounds had gone for nought and at least two pavilions had disappeared without trace. The Uffculme Cricket Club was revived in 1982 with the prospect of a permanent home at Magelake, but after a few years a shortage of players again raised doubts about its viability.

It is difficult in a short space to do justice to the fascinating story of Uffculme cricket. A longer version of these notes is available and there is a fund of anecdotes worthy of recording. For example, the late W J (John) Williams, who captained Uffculme for several seasons after 1926, and who had the keen sense of humour essential to all who aspire to lead village clubs, used to relish telling a tale that gives the true flavour of village cricket between the wars. Uffculme, returning from a match at Bampton, a club with whom they had a love-hate relationship, had stopped at their favourite hostelry for refreshment and the traditional inquest. John Williams said 'Well, we've beaten them at home at last'. To this Walt Rowsell, who was standing next to him with near empty tankard in hand, replied 'Ah, but you wouldn't have done if it hadn't been for me'. Walt was Uffculme's umpire, Uffculme's one-eyed umpire.

Sources:
UCC minute book 1926-1950
Devon and Somerset News
Notes left by the late John Adams, (1875-1962)

UFFCULME UNITED CHARITIES TRUST
by Col C W Saunders, Secretary of the Trust

ARISING from an Act of Parliament of 1815, an Uffculme Inclosure Award was made in 1838, which set aside four allotments of Charity Lands for Turbary, with parts of each reserved for the getting of stone, sand and gravel. 'Turbary' was land for the poor residing in the Parish of Uffculme to dig or cut turf for their own use, subject to the consent of the Vicar, Churchwardens and Overseers of the Parish. Stone, sand and gravel were for the Surveyors of the Highways, for making and repairing the public and private roads within the Parish.

The four allotments of land concerned are known as Uffculme Down, Gaddon Down, Slow Jacks and Hackpen Hill.

Until nearly the turn of the century the lands were used and administered as described. Then the Local Government Act of 1894 abolished the roles of 'Vicar, Churchwardens and Overseers of the Parish' and 'the Surveyors of the Highways' and transferred them to the new units of local government, in the case of Uffculme, the Parish Council.

It appears that Uffculme Parish Council did assume some or all of this responsibility, for, in a report on the Uffculme Charities in 1908 by the Charity Commissioners, it was suggested that a Charity Scheme should be established for the regulation of the property (the Charity Lands). The same report stated that the paths over the above-mentioned allotments had been maintained by the Parish Council, that the gravel pits were still in use (though only sand and stone had been taken in recent years), that there was no herbage to let and that it had been the practice for parishioners generally to resort to the allotments for recreation and shooting.

However, a formal Charity Scheme was not established until 20th October 1954, when two separate Charities, one for the Turbary Lands and one for the Stone, Sand and Gravel Lands, were made.

This scheme provided:
(a) that the lands should be administered and managed by four Trustees to be appointed (after the first appointment made by the Scheme itself) by the Parish Council.
(b) that the lands should be vested in the Official Trustee of Charity Lands (now the Official Custodian for Charities) on behalf of the Charities.
(c) that the Trustees should have the power to make regulations for the management of the Charities.

(d) that, subject to further orders of the Charity Commissioners, the Trustees were authorised to sell or lease the Turbary and the Stone, Sand and Gravel lands at Uffculme Down.

It is likely that the establishment of the Charity Scheme of 1954 came about because of the desire of quarry operators to acquire land at Uffculme Down and the discovery, then, of the inability of the Parish Council themselves to sell or lease it. Authorised sales of parts of the Uffculme Downholdings were made in 1956 and 1964. Prior to the Charity Scheme of 1954, Uffculme Parish Council had entered into a written agreement to let a portion of the Gaddon Down Allotments to James Pike. Such area of land has continued to be let to Mr William T Pike, son of James.

On the 17th March 1969, a new Charity Scheme was established for the administration and management of all the Charities in Uffculme having similar objects. The scheme, known as 'The Uffculme United Charities', renewed the powers of the Trustees over the Charity Lands, and authorised the Trustees to let and otherwise manage the lands in the Turbary and Stone, Sand and Gravel Charities not required to be retained or occupied for the purposes thereof.

The Charities coming within the jurisdiction of the Trustees, as 'Uffculme United Charities' are:
(a) a Charity consisting of Allotments for Turbary, stemming from the Uffculme Inclosure Award of 25th April 1838 and a Scheme of the Charity Commissioners of 29th October 1954.
(b) a Charity consisting of Allotments for Gravel, Stone and Sand similarly stemming.
(c) Captain James Knox's Charity, founded by the will of Catherine Knox, proved in 1837, including the subsidiary Charity of Elizabeth Ware, founded by a will proved in 1916.
(d) Anna Marker's Charity, comprised in a Declaration of Trust of 1835 and a Scheme of the Charity Commissioners in 1892.
(e) the Charity of Sarah Trott, founded by a will proved in 1905.
(f) the Charity of Margaret Walrond, founded by a will proved in 1872.

The Trustees also act as Trustees of the Charity known as Holway's and Burrough's Educational Foundation, stemming from gifts of money early in the seventeenth century by Joan Holway and Mrs Wilmot Burrough, and a Scheme of the Charity Commissioners of 1879 for 'the advancement of the education of children in the Parish of Uffculme'.

The 1969 Scheme provided that the body of Trustees to administer and manage should be seven competent persons, being one Ex-Officio Trustee, Three Nominative Trustees and Three Co-optative Trustees. The Ex-Officio Trustee is the 'Vicar for the time being of the Ecclesiastical Parish of St Mary the Virgin, Uffculme'. The Nominative Trustees are appointed by the Parish Council of Uffculme (and need not be members of the Council). The Co-optative Trustees (persons 'residing or carrying on business in or near the area of benefit') after the first appointment (by the Scheme itself) are appointed by the Trustees. The area of benefit is defined as 'the Parish of Uffculme'.

Uffculme Down looking towards Hill Head, 1854.
(from a watercolour by Peter Orlando Hutchinson).
(Devon County Record Office)

GREGORY CREASE, PHOTOGRAPHER
by Gordon Payne

FOR a small town not, until recently, a 'tourist attraction', Uffculme has provided subjects for a surprisingly large number of picture postcards.

Black and white examples from the 1920s and 1930s are of good quality and, with their glossy finishes, many have survived in fine condition. Colour postcards published in the early 1900s by L Thorne of the Post Office and R L. Mesney of Argyle Stores are obviously black and white originals tinted to give the Square an emerald green sward and Coldharbour Mill ('the Factory') some very new-looking *pink* roofs. Present-day picture postcards of the church and village with their excellent colour renderings demonstrate how far we have progressed technically, though the composition and charm of the early cards is hard to better.

A number of black and white postcards were published by Gregory Crease who lived with his wife Florence Emma in the Square. His brother Teddy was manager of the Furze Brewery at the time of its closure. A decorator by trade, Gregory was also a photographer of no mean ability.

His best photographs were in a series published in the early 1900s. They were printed on matt cream card. Though a not very durable base, it was one that provided good clear prints.

Fourteen different views in the series have been noted by the writer: the Square (south side, north side and east side), the Station, Bridge Street, Coldharbour, Bridwell Avenue, the Mill Bridge, Craddock Avenue, Fore Street, the Weir, Uffculme from Gaddon Down and from High Park and Grantlands. There may be others.

All contain interesting detail. With the aid of a magnifying glass, shops and their wares can easily be identified. Ladies in long white skirts, girls in white smocks and men carrying heavy baskets are depicted, as are numerous gas lamps, the brackets and pipework for which can still be seen. The view of lower Bridge Street is particularly interesting, showing detail of the level crossing and adjoining short semaphore signal, as well as the espalier-trained tree on the south wall of Bridge House, which still flourishes in 1988. The card of Uffculme Station is highly prized by railway 'buffs'.

Gregory Crease, with his skill and his eye for composition served us well. His pictures of Uffculme eighty-years-ago are valuable records that will increase in interest as the years pass.

Fore Street.

Bridge Street.

AN ENERGETIC PARSON:
Rev'd Henry Bramley (Vicar, 1875-1897)
by Adrian Reed

THE Rev'd Henry Bramley was probably the last of the true 'Squarsons' to hold the benefice of Uffculme. This breed of combined squire and parson, exercising both civil and spiritual authority, withered with the local government reforms of the eighteen-eighties. Uffculme, strictly speaking, had no resident 'squire'. The Clarke family, whose male heads were sometimes accorded that title, lived, in fact in the parish of Halberton although their seat, Bridwell, lay on the western edge of Uffculme. The Walronds at Bradfield were some distance away. Provided he did not antagonise either of those families, the Vicar of Uffculme had a clear field. The Rev'd Bramley seems to have made the most of it.

The roads in Uffculme frequently attracted the unfavourable comment of visitors. The Rev'd Bramley cajoled farmers into bringing marl and stones in their carts to remake Church Hill. After an initial set-back, the Vicar's road building methods proved successful and were then employed to improve the ways to Ashill and Craddock. Equally necessary was a new bridge across the Culm which could take the widest of vehicles. The Vicar set about raising money towards it. The old workshouse in Bridge Street was sold to its former Master and the almshouses were disposed of. These sales made substantial contributions to the cost of the new three-arched bridge which, with a carriage way of twenty one feet, was double that of its predecessor.

Uffculme Down then belonged to the village. The Vicar had a six-foot wide path made from the top to the bottom with seats where, as he suggested, the Women's Sewing Guild could enjoy fresh air and conversation at their meetings. His was the driving force behind the building of the Village Hall to commemorate the 1887 Royal Jubilee. To him was largely due the establishment of the first 'National' School in Uffculme.

This impressive catalogue of achievements was not completed, one imagines, without occasional friction. Nor was he *always* successful. Believing that the dead should lie near the church and not across the river, he tried to get agreement to extending the churchyard into the Rackfields to the east. He failed. At Ashill he is said to have acquired the keys of the Baptist chapel during an inter regnum and used it for his own services. However, the new minister appointed by the Baptists was a solicitor and recovered both keys and chapel. The consequence was the building of the present Anglican church of St Stephen at Ashill. Consecrated in 1882, it must be one of the few churches of the eighteen-eighties to have survived unaltered, in structure and in furnishings.

An old inhabitant of the village described the Rev'd Bramley to one of his successors as being a man who was 'into everything'. This apparently included the drinking habits of his parishioners. Any old woman he encountered setting off to an inn with an empty jug in her hand would be smartly sent home. One of them, living in the cottages south of the vicarage, tried hiding the jug under her cloak but was easily found out and turned back by the Vicar from his drive gate. To reach the London Inn which was in High Street she was compelled thereafter to make a long detour past the Leat!

UFFCULME IN 1905
An account based on a tape recording by C N (Charlie) Levett, 1894-1981

I SHOULD like to give you a little run around Uffculme as I knew it somewhere around 1905.

Now imagine we got off the half-past-four train down at Uffculme Station with the 'Puffing Billy' going—plenty of steam flying. You would be met by Mr Lake, the Station Master, a very jovial character who could be found in the evening at the Commercial Hotel (now the Ostler) having his pint. Across the way (in the Leat) were the gas works, run by Mr Walter Curwood as a private enterprise.

Well then, come out of the station and on your right lived 'Busky Churley, rising early' and next was a row of cottages which I remember being burned down shortly after. Basket-maker Staddon lived in one of the middle cottages, where the fire broke out, I believe.

Opposite, you had Harry Tapscott, another local character who ran a coal business and used to employ a young fellow called Stocker Webber who, later in life, also became quite a character. Just up the street—just before you get to the New Room (now the Village Hall) you had Shoemaker Leach, and opposite there was Tailor Hellier.

Further on the right lived Joey Venn, who was known to us boys as 'Blunderbuss Joe'. He was the gardener at the Vicarage which was on the other side of the road and if he caught any of us lads in there he fired a blunderbuss at us which kept us away for quite a while. The Vicar was Rev'd Lewis, I suppose. Rev'd Howard came along shortly after. Next door (to the vicarage) the Coxwells were in the shop on the corner. They were quite a family: Mrs Coxwell and three boys. Later on the Burdens came and took over the same shop.

Well, if you turn right and go over Fore Street, the first house on the left contained a chap called Bert Holman, who was a pioneer of the motor bike. He used to mend (push) bikes and that kind of thing but he was always fiddling with a motorbike. But, alas, he was killed in a tank in the 'fourteen War. He was a bright lad. Opposite was a butcher known as 'Porky' Luxton who kept a butcher's shop (now number two) on the corner next to the Church. Then a little way over where Gibbings' house is (now 'The Old Bakery') was Butcher Trott's. Of course, Gibbings' shop wasn't built then. That was built just after. And I suppose Coronation House (number ten, by Long's shop) went up at that time. Longs had that built but prior to that they were in the cottage opposite with their newspaper business. And next door to them, on the corner (Brook House) was Dr Burrell. And Bengal House (number fourteen) was occupied by Tommy Cottrell who was our main enemy when we went up the Hams because he owned most of the ground up there. And of course the shop facing, which is now Kimberley Snow's, (now number one, Manor House) was Polly Welland's a general grocers and sweet (shop) and one thing and another, which catered for most of the Kitwell Street area.

And down in Kitwell Street, right down at the bottom at the very end, was Parson Hicks, who lived (at Culmside) where the Brayne Bakers live now (c1978). And there was Harry Archer, our great cricketer, who got killed in the 'fourteen War; he was in Salem House. And of course, Steer's Mill, which later became Small's Mill and burned down.

Stationmaster Lake lived at Sunnybank (Kent's Close) and next up from there were the Snows. Fred Snow used to run an entire horse, taken around, you know, a stallion kind of business. And a very smart turnout that used to be.

And then you come on up Brewery Hill (East Street) and on the left the Baker's Shop (now a private house) was Curwoods. Later on he went over in the new shop (now 'The Old Bakery', Fore Street) which was built alongside where Trotts were, in that house. And next door to Curwoods, up the hill on the left, you had the back entrance to the Brewery, where you could interview most of the characters who worked there. There were 'Cap'n' Wyatt, Mr Webber, with a flowing beard, Sam Clode, Dicky Drew and, of course, if you went round the corner (near the London Inn) you came to the big noises, Ted Crease and Mr Canning. They were the big chiefs. It was known as Furze's Brewery. Of course it was a massive building. Furze's apparently had it built. In fact if you like to knock out a brick up there you will find it is stamped 'W.F.', their own bricks which, I was told, were made in Clay Lane.

If you turn right and go out Ashley Road, Mr. Wooliscroft was well installed in the School and on the left there was Mrs Chapple's private school which is now 'The Laburnums'. And just round the corner The Farmer's Hotel, where a lot of the locals used to congregate. In fact the Farmer's Hotel was noted chiefly for 'the three lights of Uffculme'—Gas Light, Electric Light and Moonlight and they comprised Albert Ware, Walter Long and Sydney Jones, who was the proprietor. I believe Sydney was 'Moonlight'. Well anyroad, he ran a saddlery bar in behind the Hotel. He had an old housekeeper called Annie Newton. There was a lot of fun in the Farmer's Arms in those days.

If you come back the other way you have the London Inn

which until recent years was occupied by the Wellands. There was 'Sir' John Welland and his father before, Phillip in the business and Albert who got killed in the 'fourteen War. He was quite a good footballer.

As you move along you come to the Williams' (now Pearce's) shop. I suppose Billy Williams' father was occupying the butcher's shop then. Across the road was another shoemaker, called Nix, and a little way up Chapel Hill yet another, called Duckham.

Well, you come along towards The Square and there was 'Little Lambscroft' where Sam Charlesworth married a Miss Mills from Gore House and moved in. Dr Eames was in 'Lambscroft' itself. Dr Eames was one of our doctors. Dr Burrell and now Dr Eames. And where Victor Welland's house is (now reconstructed) was still the family business, run by his grandfather in those days, Big John. And next door lived Nurse Clare in a cottage. On the corner was Gore House, a big house occupied by the Mills, a son and two daughters. The son became a doctor. One daughter married Sam Charlesworth and the other Canning, one of the big brewery men who lived at Prospect.

Well, going along the top of The Square you had Dr Slack, a GP who used to practice a bit of dentistry which was rather butchery, but still. I experienced it once but didn't want any more. Next door Parsons, I suppose, was the chemist, or Mesney could have been in there at the time. Mesney came along about then, anyway. And of course, the big shop, which is now the Co-op, was John Wyatt, general draper, etc. Quite a big shop.

In the two cottages down over the Square you had Postman Case in one and Tailor Manley in the other, a real local character, known as 'Hick-Me-Hoy'. Next door again, moving down towards the Church, was Miss Thorn with the Post Office, (now the National Westminster Bank) and in the back her brother ran a saddlery business. He was affectionately known as 'Assey' Thorn. He was very popular with the boys as he used to dispense fireworks down in the passage by Lloyds Bank on 5th November. He was the great fireworks man. Then you had Gregory Crease, the decorator and Miss Crease the ironmonger.

On the east side of the Square below Gore House, you had Baker Wakely and, below him, Baker Welland. Two bakers there. As you turn down around towards the Church, Lyndon House was occupied by a Mrs Woolcott and another lady. Frank Trigger, one of the local wheelwrights, lodged with them. And opposite was Fishy Gough, generally known as Fish O'Gough. And in-between there and Miss Crease was another tailor, a Mr Owen.

Coming back to the top of The Square the Commercial Hotel

The band at Grantlands, Whit Monday, 1909.

(now 'The Ostler') was kept by Mr and Mrs Peircey at the time. Here you could hire a carriage and pair. As well as any other refreshment you might have you could take a drive. Next door in the cottage lived a man called Vickery. He was a blacksmith and had a blacksmith's shop in the alleyway where the skittle alley is now. But through that yard there used to be a pathway where you could go right through to Prospect. There were three houses up there. The Curwoods, Dickinsons and Cannings lived up there.

Then across the road from the Commercial you had the Ayshford School, which was quite a school in those days, with anything from twenty to thirty boarders as well as day boys. I remember the Tracey boys from Willand attending that.

Moving along (Commercial Road) you had the chimney-sweep Kerslake in a cottage on the left (since burnt down) and then the George Hotel run by a Mr and Mrs Gorman. This was a 'modern' hotel at the time, primarily because it sported a Polyphone, where, by inserting a penny, you could have a tune of your choice. Next door in the 'Coffee Shop' (now Uffculme Men's Club) the caretaker was Mr Hannacott. The 'Coffee Shop' was a club provided for the men of Uffculme by Fox Brothers. The cottage next door was occupied by a cabinet maker named Thorn. Going back to the cottages opposite the George, I believe at that time Tailor Brice was there; yet another tailor. But, of course, he moved further over the road shortly after this period.

I can't remember exactly who occupied Osmond House at this time but, later on, Blacksmith Vickery surprised everyone by buying it and starting a bicycle shop there. But that was a few years later. Well, in the house next door lived Policeman Babb, our doyen of the peace, who looked after everything. Even Pedlar Palmer used to respect Mr Babb. Pedlar Palmer was one of the rough guys of Devon roadsters and could beat up any of them. But he never beat up Babb. I well remember the tale of how Babb gave Pedlar Palmer a good hiding up to Craddock, then took him home, gave him a good supper and sent him on the road again. But that was the way of Babb.

Well, next door there was another baker called Skanes(?). And then there was the entrance to Grantlands. Grantlands was a big estate, you see, employing seven or eight gardeners and the same number of servants. It was kept by the Bennetts in those days. Oh, quite an estate that was, looked after; the gardens were beautiful.

And over at Beech House the Thornes lived. That would be the father who we knew as 'Prickle' Thorne. 'Prickle' as a young man used to have a rifle range in the garden and we boys used to go over rifle shooting with him. He used to instruct us. Then we come on to the premises later occupied by 'Snippy' Brice (Upcott House). Of course, they were the real tailors. They employed several men. That was a different tale.

At one time there was a cottage in the garden of Upcott House. I believe some people called Jones lived there. It got burned down. Then you come to where Batstone used to live. He was a bit of a tinsmith, etc. But I am not sure if Dicky Gamlin didn't come there and have a carpenters shop. It was about that time.

I can't remember who lived in around College Court in those days. The Manse was not built then. Parson Hicks ran the Congregational Chapel and he lived right down below Steer's Mill. He had a long way to go.

Mr Hannacott had the shop at the top of Coldharbour but he used to deck out all three windows. He was a bit of a watchmaker and used to mend watches. Mrs Hannacott ran groceries and served ironmongery, pots and pans and all sorts. Mr Hannacott was the same man who used to look after the 'Coffee Shop'.

Well, then you went down Coldharbour which was mostly Fox's. One very notable person was William Andrews, one of the gentleman poachers of the time. He could get a pheasant where somebody else wouldn't think of them. He was linked up with Sammy Sparkes who was the son of old man Sparkes who was the Manager of the Fox's down at the bottom at the time. And, of course, Sammy and William would get up to these capers. Of course, Bill Andrews was one of the big noises at the Factory really. But prior to that there was George Woodgates who eventually became Manager. Bill Andrews died young. Sammy Sparkes I believe died recently. He would have been well over ninety if alive.

There was a blacksmith, a real character, in Fore Street, who I missed, called Tom Hayward. He was a patron of the Commercial and also looked after the Church, was the Verger and all that kind of thing. We called him one of the lads of the village. He lined up with the 'three lights of Uffculme', I suppose, in those days.

Down in Coldharbour, a couple I missed were Fred Hurford and John Adams, both of them with a kind of reporting flair. John Adams was quite a historian of all Uffculme. I suppose he had more knowledge of old Uffculme than anyone of his generation. Fred Hurford used to be the correspondent for the local papers. He had a fair knowledge of everything going on. Both have been dead some time.

Of course, if you scout along to the local gentry and go out around a bit you go up to Craddock. In the Cleeve, I believe, Chestermans used to live and of course (in) Craddock House was the New family, the old man New with his sons. Latterly Harry New came into that. He was a debatable figure in the locality. He was a big councillor and fought hard for the water scheme in later years.

Coming back into Uffculme, Teddy Crease had a new house built near Uffculme Downs. He used to drive his horse and carriage and one thing and another. He was boss of the brewery and when it closed he went off and joined Starkey, Knight and Ford at Tiverton. He was a brother of (Gregory) Crease, the painter and decorator.

Then you go up to 'Mount View', which is now 'Poynings', and up there you have Mr de Paer(?). He followed the Furzes in. He was a great accountant in London and used to go off on Monday mornings and come home Friday nights, with his carriage and pair to meet him off the train at Tiverton Junction and drive either up the main road and in, or, sometimes, through Uffculme and up Clay Lane and through the okeway where his coach driver lived—up in the corner through the archway.

And at Bridwell there was Richard Hall Clarke, one of the old-time gentlemen who lived a quiet life there. Down at Mountstephen you had Billy Tanner. Now he was a well-known cricketer for Uffculme and kept wicket. I believe he kept wicket after Walter Long, one of the 'lights' of Uffculme.

A couple of shops I left out. Right opposite the George, next to Tailor Brice, in the Cottages there, was a little shop kept by a Miss Wyatt, a rather elderly lady. It was a sweet shop, mainly, and sold gobstoppers which we used to think were wonderful.

Another shop down at the bottom of Coldharbour on the right was kept by the Graves. Mabel Graves taught at Uffculme School. She used to perform with Miss Florrie Woolcott of those days—on the infants' side under Mrs. Corner. There were two sons of the Graves family. One, Herbie Graves, played football for Uffculme in the olden days and the other was the blacksmith, Dapper Graves. Dapper was, in those days, an apprentice with John Hayward, so you can guess that as a local character he had a good training. No matter where you went if people asked for Uffculme, they would always ask for Dapper Graves.

> The above notes are not verbatim but they contain most of what Mr Levett recorded, in or about 1978. The additions, in brackets, are to help identify the properties referred to.
>
> E J Gollop

A VISITOR'S VIEW OF UFFCULME IN 1849
by Adrian Reed

'This place must be situated either at the north or the south pole, since every other place moves forward but Uffculme seems to stand still. There is a great lack of public spirit there, and even of morality among the lower orders. Since the death of Mr Clarke, of Bridwell, there has been but one magistrate in the parish; and as he numbers nearly four score years, he is either too good or too aged to cope with garden robbers and other depredators. The roads are neglected, and people forget the duties which they owe to themselves. If you take a walk in the neighbourhood, or go to Church on Sunday, you are in danger of getting ankle-deep in mud. Why are not some of the gentry elected to the position of magistrates?

The air of the place is bracing and healthy, and the scenery through the valley of the Culme in picturesque; but what inducement have strangers to take up their residence where so little is done to allure them? A physician, practicing at one of the watering places on the south coast, recently applied to know whether there was a respectable lodging in Uffculme, with a view to recommending some of his patients a change of air, but the reply to this question was 'No'! If Uffculme does not thrive whose fault is it?'

THIS unsigned article, which appeared in *Woolmer's Exeter and Plymouth Gazette* for 17th March 1849 was, in fact, written by Peter Orlando Hutchinson, the Sidmouth antiquary, who noted in his diary: 'It (the article) reflects on their dirty roads, neglect of their local duties, and public spirit. There is nothing like a paragraph in a newspaper to make people look about'.

Hutchinson was a close, if critical, observer of the Uffculme scene, forming his impressions during visits to his cousins, the Rev'd Francis Jones, Master of the Grammar School, and his wife Marianne, between 1847 and 1854. A middle-aged bachelor, he seems to have been a welcome guest, especially with the five (later six) Jones children and was once left in charge of them, and the four maids, while the parents were away. He claimed that they returned just in time to prevent the declaration of a juvenile republic!

To get to Uffculme from Sidmouth, Hutchinson had to travel by stage coach to Exeter, by rail to Tiverton Junction and then by fly to the village. Not surprisingly, his stays were generally two or three months long. Much of his time seems to have been spent in reading or, when the weather allowed, in walking and watercolour sketching. He was a meticulous draughtsman and has left valuable records of contemporary Uffculme in his sketch books which are now deposited in the Devon Record Office in Exeter. In these are views of the old town bridge over the Culm, one of which shows that it must have been too narrow for wheeled traffic of any size and was intended mainly for pack-horses. There are two passing bays for pedestrians on each side and four arches compared to the three of its successor. Alongside the bridge is the well rutted approach to the ford which was the usual crossing placed for waggons. Another view drawn from upstream, beside the stone built outflow of the corn mill leat, was at the cost of a severe cold from sitting on damp March grass while making it.

SMITHINCOT BRIDGE, OVER THE CULM, UFFCULME.

(Devon County Record Office)

The bridge at Smithincott, drawn in more agreeable weather, was then a simple footbridge supported by a trestle in mid-stream. There is a cottage beside it and plenty of trees. In fact, one of the main impressions Hutchinson's sketches give is that of a well-wooded countryside and a village equally well provided with shady trees. The church had only just had its major restoration completed, including the rebuilding of the tower and the addition of the steeple. He found it 'unusually handsome for a small country town' and made a number of drawings of the monuments in it. Naturally, he painted the Grammar School and the view he took of its east side shows little change from that seen today. See page 22.

As an antiquarian he made determined efforts to discover the legendary 'Pixie Garden' on Uffculme Down. Finally, he traced an old man who told him that it had been levelled by ploughing after the area was enclosed at the beginning of the century. The old man assured him that he had played in it as a child, when it was considered lucky to jump over the two-foot earth walls of which it was formed. Hutchinson had to content himself with an unlikely looking plan in his diary, based on what he had been told, and a delightful watercolour of the field in which it was supposed to have been. See page 96.

More rewarding was a walk in September 1854 to Blackborough and Punchy Down. Here, on the borders of the three parishes of Uffculme, Sheldon and Kentisbeare, were the greenstone workings in the so-called Whetstone Hills. He drew a whetstone cutter as work, seated, his left knee protected by a thick pad. He was trimming the greenstone with a tool resembling a small double-headed battle axe, but with the short handle at right angles to the blades. To the left of the man is the timber-shored entrance to one of the horizontal adits running up to three hundred yards into the hillside. The industry was killed by the introduction of imported and far cheaper Carborundum as a sharpener for tools. The miners, who were not local, dispersed. R D Blackmore in his novel 'Perlycross' (Culmstock) describes something of the way in which they lived according to their own self-made laws. See page 113.

On this same excursion, Hutchinson visited and recorded the remains of Garnsey's Tower, Uffculme's only Romantic Age folly. Today it is a pile of rubble only a few feet high in the wood about half a mile north-east of Blackborough church. In 1854, Hutchinson described it as a 'circular tower three stories high though floors are ruined and fallen down with traces of fire places—walls two feet thick but cracked from top to bottom—windows blocked up to strengthen the building, nevertheless so tottering that it threatens to fall'. He measured it as being twelve feet in diameter and from the figures drawn standing at its base in his sketch its height then would seem to have been about thirty to thirty five feet. Presumably it was even taller before the roof fell in.

This folly is of some interest as it does not seem to have been built, as were most, by a nobleman to embellish his estate. The Garnseys were modest if well-to-do country gentlemen living at

Bodmiscombe. Local tradition suggests that the tower was the work of the two brothers, John and Thomas Garnsey, who bought the manor of Bodmiscombe in 1791 for over £6,900, a substantial sum in those days. Both died bachelors, John, the survivor, sometime in the 1840s. One of Hutchinson's sketches, a view from Uffculme Down, shows the top of the tower rising above the trees although it had, by then, lost whatever kind of roof it may have had. When first completed, anyone standing on that roof would have been able to look through three hundred and sixty degrees for distances of forty miles or more.

Garnsey's Tower, Blackborough Hill. — Coloured there Sep. 12. 1854. There are the remains of two floors inside this tower, a staircase and two fire places. The walls are two feet thick, the diameter of the building 12 feet; but so cracked and ruinous, as to threaten great risk of falling.

(Devon County Record Office)

After the Joneses left the Grammar School, Hutchinson had no reason to revisit Uffculme and so to modify his attitude to the village and its inhabitants. He looked upon it and them as forming a community having little contact with the outside world. Indeed, he described a visit in March 1849 of 'Wombwells itinerant collection of animals' as 'a kind of sight that had never before greeted this retired place. The Uffculmers were stricken with extreme wonderment when the elephant walked into the market-place with a lady riding on his back, seated in a houda.' Such evidences of the outside world no doubt became more frequent after the railway reached Uffculme, though an elephant in the Square would probably still not pass unnoticed today!

(Devon County Record Office)

GAP 1988

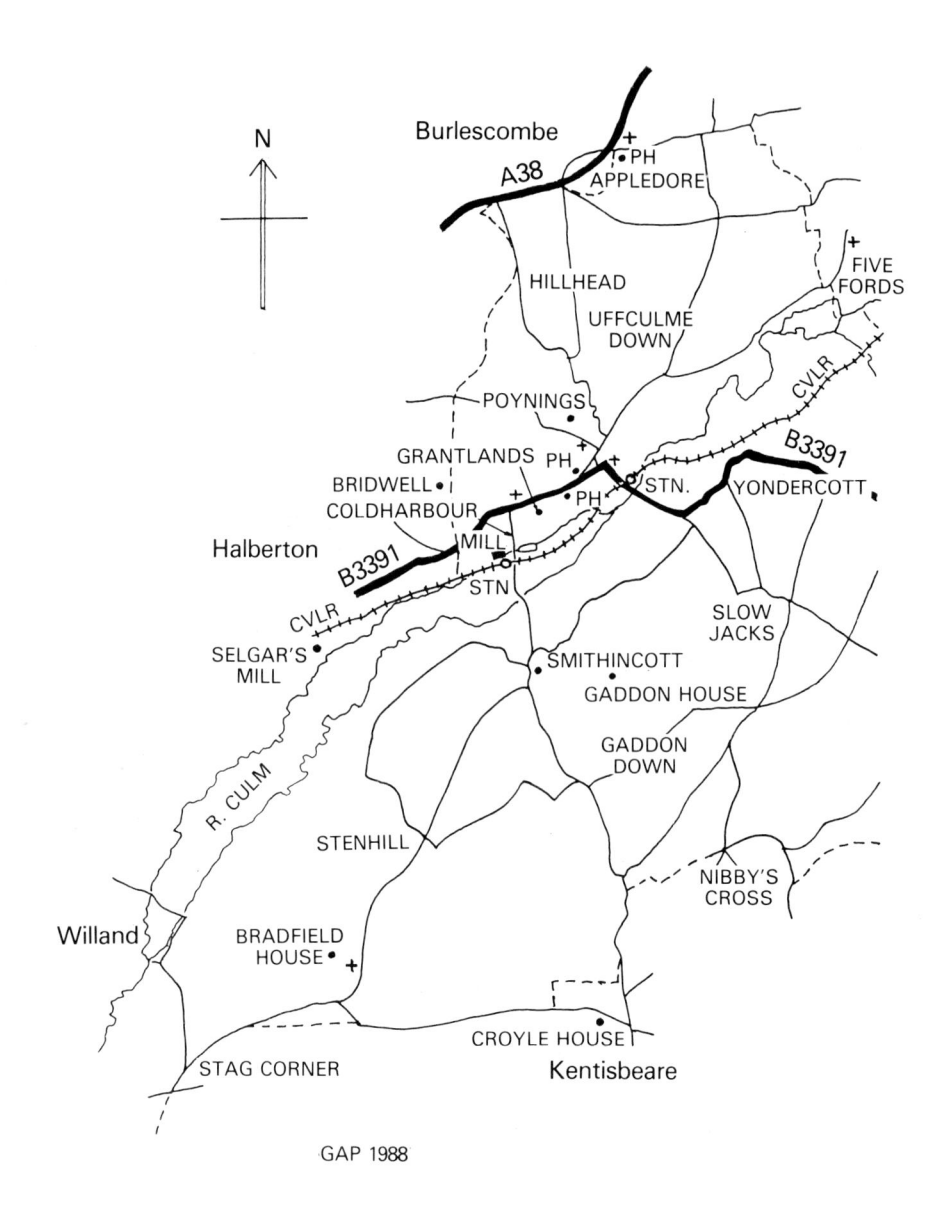

NOTES

Further copies of this book may be obtained from:
ULHG
11a Grantlands
Uffculme
Devon EX15 3ED

Price £5.00 (post free).

Please include remittance payable to 'Uffculme Local History Group' with your order.